Night Vision

From 2003 to 2008, Jon Oliver was chaplain to the nightclubs in Bournemouth, during which time he regularly stayed up long past his bed-time, while exploring the possibilities of church and mission among those who live, work and play in the nightlife. Shortly after he finished writing this book, Jon moved to Cambridge and began training for ordination in the Church of England.

Night Vision

Mission adventures in
club culture and the nightlife

Jon Oliver

Forewords by
Andy Hunter and Graham Cray

CANTERBURY
PRESS
Norwich

© Jon Oliver and the contributors 2009

First published in 2009 by the Canterbury Press Norwich
Editorial office
13–17 Long Lane,
London, EC1A 9PN, UK

Canterbury Press is an imprint of Hymns Ancient and Modern Ltd
(a registered charity)
St Mary's Works, St Mary's Plain,
Norwich, NR3 3BH, UK

www.scm-canterburypress.co.uk

British Library Cataloguing in Publication data

A catalogue record for this book is available
from the British Library

ISBN 978-1-85311-956-9

Typeset by Regent Typesetting, London
Printed in the UK by
CPI William Clowes Beccles NR34 7TL

For Helen

Contents

Bible Versions and Abbreviations

Unless otherwise indicated, scripture quotations are taken from the Holy Bible, Today's New International Version®. Copyright © 2001, 2005 by International Bible Society®. Used by permission of International Bible Society®. All rights reserved worldwide. 'TNIV' and 'Today's New International Version' are trademarks registered in the United States Patent and Trademark Office by International Bible Society®. Use of either trademark requires the permission of International Bible Society.

Scripture quotations marked AMP are taken from The Amplified Bible, Old Testament copyright © 1965, 1987 by the Zondervan Corporation. The Amplified New Testament copyright © 1958, 1987 by The Lockman Foundation. Used by permission.

Scripture quotations marked JBP are taken from The New Testament in Modern English. Copyright © by J.B. Phillips, 1960, 1972. Revised edition published by Fount Paperbacks, London.

Scripture quotations marked MSG are taken from The Message. Copyright © by Eugene H. Peterson, 1993, 1994, 1995. Used by permission of NavPress Publishing Group.

Scripture quotations marked NIV are taken from the Holy Bible, New International Version®. Copyright © 1973, 1978, 1984 International Bible Society. Used by permission of Zondervan. All rights

Acknowledgements

There are, of course, too many people for me to be able to mention everyone, but in particular I would like to offer grateful thanks to my management committee – David, Helen, Jim, Lloydie, Rob and Ron – and to all the others who have supported me as nightclub chaplain, for encouraging and believing in me (and for paying me!); to Jonny Baker, Aaron Gibson, Chris Harwood, Gaz Kishere, Steve Leach and Simon Oliver, for their wisdom, insight, challenge and inspiration; to Mum and Dad, for the food, the love, the genes, and for letting me sit in their shed to write the first draft of this book; and to my many wonderful friends, for providing support, encouragement, alcohol and laughter at all the right times.

I would also like to say an enormous thank you to everyone who contributed to this book, for giving so generously of their time and their stories.

And finally, thank you God, for obvious reasons.

David danced before the LORD with all his might; with shouts and the sounds of trumpets, he leapt and danced before the Lord.

2 Samuel, chapter 6

The dance of God represents a flowing movement of the divine nature. Through the work of the Spirit in and upon the believer, he or she is allowed to participate in this divine life. This can be likened to a kind of 'progressive dance', a dance where the participants move outside of the original circle and invite others to join in the pattern of their movement. So it is also with the divine story of the dancers. The divine dance of Father, Son, and Holy Spirit draws us into their energizing and invigorating movement. In our worship and in our mission we participate in the intimate life of God.

Pete Ward, *Liquid Church*

Forewords

As Christians, we are called to be the salt and the light wherever and whenever we find ourselves; we are supposed to bring out the God-flavours and God-colours in this world. A lot of the time we mistakenly think that in order to achieve this we need to be constantly telling people about Jesus, and we don't realize sometimes just being there can say far more, that the fingerprints of God in our lives can speak volumes in today's culture.

There have been times when I have been in a club playing my music and people have come up to me and said that I bring a different atmosphere – someone once said that I had the hand of God on my life – and all this before I even open my mouth.

Clubland is a place that Christians often shy away from; we worry that it will affect us, that we will be tarnished by it and by what goes on. Along with many others, Jon and I believe that the opposite is true, that God is bigger than all of this, all of culture. This book is full of stories which show that this is the case, which tell of Christians being the salt and the light in a culture where, just like in the rest of the world, people desperately need to experience the flavour of God in their lives.

Andy Hunter
DJ & Producer

It has taken most of my lifetime for the church in the UK to learn that Christ did not command us to get people to 'come to' church as we like it, but to 'go to' people, to embody and gossip the gospel where they are, and to plant transformative gospel communities in each culture.

This book is an interim report from some pioneers who have been following Jesus' command in the nightclub scene, which has dominated Britain's youth and young adult culture for more than 20 years.

It is an interim report because most of these stories are stories of missionary obedience taken one step at a time, rather than of plans fulfilled. It is a significant report because missionary engagement with much of our diverse culture is likely to be through such faith and obedience. The day of missionary blueprints is over.

Note that these pioneer missionaries are not necessarily cross-cultural missionaries. Many of them are people called to a culture in which they grew up. It is when they relate to inherited church that they have to be cross-cultural! Others have heard the call of God to a culture that was not native to them. Club culture is not monochrome, nor are the missionaries God sends. A variety of approaches is described here. Each was worked out contextually and, as such, they are not models to imitate but examples of processes of local discernment, to enrich our imaginations as we engage with our context. As I read them I was struck by the importance of community – solo mission is a dangerous and vulnerable strategy – and by the centrality of prayer – including 24/7. I was equally struck by the quality of pastoral patience, by a willingness to hear God call time on a project when its time had come, and by a continual openness to God's future.

If you are considering engaging in club or nightlife ministry, here is an excellent primer. If you are called to a different missionary context, you will find inspiration for your step-by-step faith and obedience.

Graham Cray
Bishop of Maidstone and Chair of the
Mission-Shaped Church Report

Introduction

We've heard rumours that the church is dying. We've read claims that Christianity has little relevance in contemporary society. We've seen statistics suggesting that fewer and fewer people are interested in faith. We've witnessed the steady decline in attendance at Sunday services. We've watched in dismay as yet another evangelistic event ends in mediocrity. And deep down, we've all known that we need to do something about it – if only we could work out how.

The bizarre thing is that although the last century saw the church fall into seemingly terminal decline in the UK, the past couple of decades have seen a significant rise in spiritual openness. Everywhere I look there are signs that people are longing for something more, and questioning whether this 'something more' may need to be found outside and beyond themselves. I have found that when offered the right opportunities in the appropriate context, most people readily engage in exploring the big questions about the meaning of life and the possibility of God . . . and yet few, if any, are looking to the church for guidance or companionship in their spiritual journeys. I remain convinced that the church, as the body of Christ, has so much to offer on every conceivable level of human existence . . . and yet many, if not most, people I meet seem to consistently write off the church as an outdated and irrelevant institution.

However, there is hope. There is always hope.

We have a living hope: Jesus Christ. And everywhere I look, despite the pessimistic declarations on TV, in the papers, and even from among our own ranks, I see encouraging signs of Christ at work in the world: dynamic young (and often not-so-young) Christians coming together to join in with God's great adventure of mission in contemporary society; people recognizing the needs of those around them, and the call of God to develop an appropriate and relevant response to these needs; people willing to get among it all, to get their hands dirty, and to get alongside people in their spiritual journeys.

This dynamism is particularly evident within club culture and the nightlife. All over the UK people are developing a fresh vision for engaging with God's mission in this culture – from clubbers and DJs to pastors and evangelists, in the clubs and on the streets, full time, part time, any time. What makes this so exciting is that there is such breadth to this cultural landscape, and such variety and creativity in the approaches people have found to respond to this challenge. The club scene is so diverse and transient that there simply is no 'right way' to go about this task – in every context there is a different way to join in with this same mission.

In my work as chaplain to the nightclubs in Bournemouth, I have explored a variety of approaches to this mission – from organizing teams to go into specific clubs on specific nights, to running our own club night in a late-night bar, from taking teams on to the streets around the clubs at weekends, to opening a big town centre church all night and inviting clubbers in. This shows that even with just one group of people working in one town, there is huge scope for diversity. I will share more of my journey with you later, but I don't just want to tell my own tale in this book – instead, I have collected together stories from all sorts of people working in different ways and in different places. So, after a few chapters discussing the nature of mission, club culture and contemporary spirituality, this book is filled with accounts written by others involved in this mission in club culture and the nightlife. Let me introduce the people who have contributed their stories:

Greg Bartlem is possibly the least likely pioneer you will ever meet. He's into 80s music, he used to front a series of *Dr Who* conventions, and he's never been cool in his life – although he says you never miss what you never had! Despite this résumé, Greg's job is to help church congregations build links with the young people who gather outside their church buildings, and the last few years have seen him develop a variety of pioneering ministries among young people and clubbers in Coventry city centre.

Dave Cates spent over ten years in the club scene, reaching out to clubbers and leading a small, mission-focused community in Sheffield, which loved, served and made disciples within the night-life. Dave says that he's often looked at the church and thought, 'There must be more than this . . .'! Although he's seen and belonged to some amazing churches, he's still looking for more – never standing still, always looking to God, always seeking out new adventures, always expecting the next step of faith to freak the pants off him more than the last, and desperately wanting people to really 'get' how much God loves them.

Lorraine Dixon (aka DJ Ayo) is an Anglican priest, a pioneer missioner, and a DJ. At the core of her ministry are the various club nights she promotes, which she describes as an attempt to reach out, in mutual love of the music, to the young adults who are part of Birmingham's dance music scene. Lorraine is passionate about music – she loves going to other club nights in the city, is currently studying for an MA in Music, and in her spare time plays the violin in a string orchestra. Lorraine is married to Steven Bird, who gives her much support and encouragement in all she does.

Ant Newman has been involved with various mission and outreach projects in his time – including many years spent leading a vibrant community of Christians who are creatively and holistically involved in the Southampton club scene. He DJs and produces drum & bass, loves breakdancing and body-popping, and was privileged to be part of the 24-7 Prayer mission team in Ayia Napa for several years. Ant lives and works in Southampton, where he supports those with substance and alcohol misuse problems, and describes himself as a highly dysfunctional person saved by Jesus on a daily basis.

Jon Oliver originally moved to the south coast for a few months, but loved it so much that he stayed for nearly a decade – for the last few years working as chaplain to the nightclubs in Bournemouth. One of his favourite memories from this time was going to a massive cave rave organized by a local promoter in a disused quarry dug into the top of a worryingly high cliff-face. Jon struggles to wake up before lunchtime, loves the fact that he hardly ever has to queue to get into a club, and feels funny writing about himself in the third person!

Graham Robinson (aka Shakinda) is from Belfast, and started going clubbing when he was fifteen. He says that a few years after this, Jesus 'hijacked him with love' and they started hanging out together – and ever since he's been trying to communicate that love within the clubbing community. Graham has recently taught himself the art of VJing, allowing him to present scripture and prophecy to clubbers in a unique way, and is enormously grateful to God for the opportunities that have opened up for him to VJ for some of the world's top clubs and DJs – from Ministry of Sound to Miami, Armin van Buuren to Pete Tong.

Doug Ross (aka Kubiks) has a lot of fingers in a lot of pies. As well as being a DJ and a music producer, he has also set up a successful club night in Bristol (The Rubiks Cube), established a small record label to promote new artists (Rubik Records), and currently runs an artists/events management agency (Spilt Milk Bookings). After God, his family, and music, Doug's biggest passion in life is cooking – his home-cooked Thai green curry in particular has assumed legendary status. Recently he's been getting into reggae-influenced dub music, and says the deep basslines and sweeping vocals make him feel as if it's always summertime.

Sarah Smith loves to dance. She also loves God, and for several years combined these two great loves by heading up a 24-7 Prayer team touring various clubs in central London. Sarah also loves to travel, and is currently combining this with her passion for educating young people on sexual health issues, by volunteering as an HIV/ AIDS educator in Mbale, Uganda. She says that one of her most memorable nights out was at the superclub Privilege, where she bravely traversed a precariously narrow walkway above an indoor swimming pool – just to give a thank-you card to the DJ.

Gavin Tyte (aka TyTe) has been dubbed 'The Yoda of Beatbox' and has been instrumental in creating the global phenomenon that is human beatboxing. For several years he ran the website humanbeatbox.com, where his online tutorials helped a generation of beatboxers get started in this art form. He is also an Anglican priest. Gavin loves both fishing and huge sound systems, and has become famous for his 'Scooby Doo versus The Daleks' beatbox battle routine. He currently lives and works in Bath with his wife Lucy and their two daughters, seeking to transform a community with the love of Jesus.

Dave Ward started his working life as a farrier (shoeing horses) and came to know Christ when he was twenty-five, partly due to a tree branch falling on his washing shortly after he'd been swearing at God for allowing it to rain three solid days in a row, during a seven-month tour of Europe in a VW van. A couple of years later Dave went into full-time youth work, and these days he heads up the Malt Cross café-bar in Nottingham city centre. He is married to Deb and has four children, who keep his feet firmly on the ground.

Vicky Ward has been involved in the 24-7 Prayer movement ever since the dream first became a reality in the back room of a church in Chichester, and is still part of the 24-7 Prayer UK team. Originally from Portsmouth, she has been working with homeless people in Sheffield for several years. Vicky was heavily involved in the adventures of 24-7 Prayer in Ibiza for many years and, although she's no longer part of this team, she still loves to dance, dance, dance – and can usually be found twirling her way round local bars and clubs at the weekend.

My vision for this book is simply to give an eclectic overview of the many and varied ways in which people have joined in with God's mission in club culture and the nightlife. I think everyone who has contributed their stories would admit that they haven't found the 'answer', that none of us have found the 'right way' or 'only way' to engage in this mission. Nevertheless, we hope you will gain something from our collected experiences, our successes and failures, our insights, hindsights and foresights. There are, however, a few things to mention before you read on:

- This isn't a 'How to . . .' book. The idea isn't to tell you how to do it, but to show you how some people have done it. Rather than reflecting simply one person's perspective, I thought it would be more valuable to offer you the opportunity to read about, and hopefully learn from, a wide variety of perspectives. The aim is not to promote a particular model or way of doing things, but to inspire you to develop your own ideas and approaches.
- I'm not an expert. If you want an in-depth analysis of musical, cultural or global trends in the club scene, I'm the wrong person to ask! There are plenty of people who could tell you many interesting and insightful things about it all (some of whom have contributed their stories to this book), but I'm just a simple chap who loves people, loves clubbing and loves God.
- This is definitely not the last word on the matter – or even *my* last word on the matter. This is a small selection of the innumerable stories that could have been included – and I'm sure that if you look around you'll find many others with their own tales to tell about their mission adventures in club culture and the nightlife.

Whoever you are – whether you're already involved in this form of mission, contemplating the possibilities or simply interested in exploring mission in contemporary culture – my hope and prayer is that you will find something within these pages to encourage and inspire you.

The Mission of God

JON OLIVER

Whenever I look through my Bible, I am soon reminded that God is revealed in its pages as a God of mission. From walking with Adam in the garden of Eden, to calling Abraham to father his holy nation, from assuming human form to reveal God to humanity, to sending the Holy Spirit to help us do the same – the Bible consistently shows us a missionary God. From beginning to end, the Bible speaks of a God of mission. In fact, until a few hundred years ago, the Latin word *missio* (from which we get the word 'mission') was used exclusively to describe the action of the Trinity, denoting the sending of the Son and the Holy Spirit into the world.[1]

So let's get this clear from the start: when we talk about mission, we're talking about the mission of God, the *missio Dei*. As Jürgen Moltmann says, 'It is not the church that has a mission of salvation to fulfil in the world; it is the mission of the Son and the Spirit through the Father that includes the church.'[2] Mission is not an activity of the church but an attribute of God,[3] his movement in and towards the world. I have no doubt that he could do a great job without us, that he could proclaim the good news using lifeless stones if it suited his purposes, but in God's bizarre logic he chooses to use us. In his infinite wisdom, he calls us to join him in his mission.

So what is this mission?

From the very beginning, from that first call to Adam, 'Where are you?' (Genesis 3.9), the Bible can be viewed as one long story of God searching us out, trying to get our attention, inviting us back into a relationship with him, our beautiful, generous, loving Father. This is God's mission – his glorious movement towards humanity, full of love, full of grace, and overflowing with gifts from his rich and abundant treasure-house.

Our calling is to respond to join this movement, to join in with God's mission, to go into all the world and make disciples of all nations; to love unconditionally, to strive for justice and mercy, to see lives transformed, and to invite humanity back into relationship with God. For 2,000 years the church has responded to this call to take the good news into the whole world, seeing Christianity grow from its humble beginnings as an obscure Jewish sect into a world-wide community of faith. If you think about it, there is only church because there is mission. As Emil Brunner says, 'The church exists by mission, just as fire exists by burning.'[4] And if the church is declining in the Western world, surely this is largely due to our failure to engage fully with the mission of God.

I admit that in the face of ridicule or indifference from the world at large, it can be tempting to hide away, to play quietly in the corner, in the relative safety of our own little gatherings, in our 'holy huddles' or 'church ghettos'. But mission is not an optional extra, an add-on, an upgrade to the standard-model Christian life. It's an absolute essential. The Bible doesn't just speak of a missionary God, it speaks of a missionary *church*, and it calls us to become a missionary people.

Are you in?

God is calling out to us to be his partners in mission, to take the good news into the whole world. And let's remember that this is *good* news. This is the unbelievably good news that God so loved the world, and was so desperate to be in relationship with us, that he sent his Son to live, die and rise for us. This is the absolutely fantastic news that God runs to meet us in the midst of our mess, in the centre of our suffering, with the assurance that there is hope for us yet. This is the outstandingly, extravagantly, superlatively spectacular news of Jesus – because Jesus himself is the good news, the pinnacle of human experience, the high-point of God's mission in the world. And we are commissioned to pass on this good news with all our being: 'All authority in heaven and on earth has been given to me. Therefore go and make disciples of all nations' (Matthew 28.18–19).

However unfathomable it may seem, Jesus wants to use us in getting this good news out to other people too. *Me?* A lazy little blighter, an impertinent young scamp, a dirty little sinner, an ordinary human being (called and redeemed by God, but still flawed). He wants to use *me?*

Come on!

This is the ultimate invitation – the creator of the universe is calling on every single one of us to join his great mission in the world. Let's get some. Let's get in among it. Let's get our hands dirty. This is life in all its fullness. Living for God, following his lead, seeking him out and joining his great adventure. Mike Riddell described this mission as 'an open river which flows where it will, into which we may plunge if we have courage enough'.[5] This is an invitation to dive in. This is an invitation to join in with the adventure of a lifetime. Can you think of anything more exciting, essential or worthwhile? Are you in? This is too good to be missed. It really is.

So what do we do?

Ha!

I'm not so sure.

I used to worry about this. I used to think it was all about talking to people about Jesus and, growing up in church, I lost count of the number of times I was told that this is what I should do. But it seemed that whenever I tried to start a conversation about Jesus, I would end up tongue-tied and stumbling over my words. I really did want other people to know about the good news, but somehow this beautiful ideal always seemed to be reduced to uncomfortable conversations.

Not to be put off so easily, I went on various mission trips and summer teams, took a year out to work as a missionary in Africa, and a couple of times I even went along with a bunch of people doing street preaching. Whenever it came to outreach time, we'd be sent out with the expectation that we should come back with half a dozen converts in tow. But no matter how many of these things I got involved with, most of the time I still didn't really know what I was supposed to be doing. Or rather I knew *what* I was supposed to be doing (coming back with half a dozen converts in tow), I just didn't know *how*. And that made me worried – so usually I'd just shy away, hide at the back of the crowd or, at best, stand behind someone who was a little less scared than me, nodding along with whatever they were saying. I knew I should get more involved – I honestly wanted to – I just didn't know how. So all too often I'd end up doing nothing. Then I'd feel guilty, which made me even more worried. And it seemed to me that at this rate I was never going to get anywhere or help anyone.

How I learnt to stop worrying:

First, I realized I didn't have to blurt everything out at every opportunity. I realized we don't have to bulldoze everyone we meet with an instant rendition of Jesus' life-story within a framework of the wider biblical narrative, complete with a systematic summary of Christian doctrine, alongside an exegetical outworking of our own particular denomination's statement of faith, and an overview of the theological issues facing the contemporary church, perhaps with a sprinkling of bias of our own unique recipe, all wrapped up with an altar-call invitation to give their lives to Jesus! Let's face it, if we expect everyone we talk to about Jesus to drop down on their knees, accepting him as their Lord and Saviour, as likely as not we'll soon end up pretty disappointed and eventually pretty disillusioned.

In my experience, far too much of our evangelistic energy seems to focus on an event, a particular moment, with the underlying assumption that conversion occurs at a specific point in time. The problem with this assumption is that the majority of Christians can't actually pinpoint such a moment. Dave Tomlinson says, 'A recent survey of how people find faith showed that 69 per cent of people cannot put a date on their conversion: it was a gradual process – a journey . . . the average time is about four years.'[6] Recently I met a woman who had become a Christian after a long time spent on the darker fringes of club culture – and while she may have been able to name the date she had consciously given her life to Jesus, she could also trace her journey back over ten years, beginning with a conversation she had with a bunch of Christians offering bottles of water to dehydrated clubbers outside a nightclub in Bradford. It occurred to me that even when people try to identify a specific conversion experience, rarely will it have been quite this sudden – it's likely God will have been working in their lives for some time. So perhaps, as a friend of mine once suggested, the aim of any evangelistic encounter is simply to leave people more positively disposed to the gospel, ready for their next encounter with a Christian.

As I came to understand both life and faith as an ongoing journey of discovery, I realized that for the Christian experience truly to resonate with people, it needs to be part of this journey – and that evangelism focusing primarily on a single, specific moment in time is not sufficient. As I thought about the fact that I've never felt particularly gifted in this sort of evangelism, it dawned on me that I am nevertheless pretty good at caring for people pastorally, getting alongside them in their darkness and struggles, and that I'm quite good at teaching, helping people in their search for meaning and understanding. More importantly, I realized these skills were my valid contributions to the wider task of the church. St Paul said that some people are given to be apostles, some to be prophets, some to be evangelists, some to be pastors and teachers (Ephesians 4.11). I fit in somewhere near the end of that list. In other words, I'm not an evangelist. Maybe you are – that's brilliant! Maybe you're not – that's OK too! As Christians, our whole lives should be inherently evangelistic – but this is not necessarily about out-and-out Evangelism with a capital 'E'.

If we acknowledge that mission is God's movement in and towards the world – the sending forth of the Son, the Spirit and the Church – it becomes clear that evangelism focusing on proclaiming the gospel and seeking conversion is only one aspect of the wider mission. Evangelism is mission, but mission is far more than evangelism. Proclamation and conversion are vitally important – we have been commissioned to preach the gospel to all creation and to make disciples of all nations (Mark 16.15; Matthew 28.18–19) –

but our calling is to much more than this. We are called not only to preach the gospel, but to live it.

After all, Jesus didn't just preach the good news, he *was* the good news.

What would Jesus do?

There are many aspects of Jesus' life that have had a real impact on my understanding of mission over the years, but I would like to look at just a few of them here – first and foremost, the very nature of the Incarnation. Jesus didn't turn up riding on the clouds with a choir of angels at his side; rather he set aside the privileges of being one with God, embraced humanity, and moved into the neighbourhood (John 1.14, MSG). As Cathy Kirkpatrick says, 'God shows up on our turf, speaking our language so that we might understand.'[7]

It's easy to get so familiar with this story that we forget how phenomenal it is – God, the creator and sustainer of the universe, turning up here, on earth, as one of us. Not only that, but he made his life among us. He may have gone off to pray by himself sometimes, but usually he was right in the thick of things. He may have taught in the temple on occasions, but mostly he was out in the real world, dealing with real people and real situations. He lived his life among people: travelling with them, eating with them, laughing with them, mourning with them. And his whole life was so attractive, his teachings and actions so astounding, that in no time his fame spread and thousands of people were searching him out.

I am convinced that one of the things that most attracted these crowds to Jesus was that he cared for people holistically – body, mind and spirit. He didn't simply preach sermons or lay down dogmatic statements telling people what to do, but demonstrated the way through his own life and example. He helped, healed and fed people; he comforted the bereaved, opposed injustice, and spoke out for the voiceless; he engaged with political and religious leaders, challenged authority and hypocrisy, crossed social and cultural boundaries, undermined certainty and religious self-congratulation, demonstrated supreme self-sacrifice; and – above all else – he showed love, real love, endless, all-consuming, unconditional love.

No wonder such huge crowds were so desperate to seek him out. Many of those who did track him down found him so irresistible they followed him wherever he went, some of them giving up all they owned, leaving everything behind, so they could always be with him. Others found him deeply disturbing, largely because he challenged and flaunted the religious norms of the day – consistently spending time with sinners, with the outsiders and rejects of society, people who were considered unclean and unworthy by the religious authorities. According to St Luke, Jesus had an unrelenting agenda towards the least, the last and the lost. He did spend time with the rulers and leaders, but he didn't pay them any special attention because of their status – if anything, he treated them more harshly for abusing their positions of power and authority. Throughout his ministry Jesus continually blurred boundaries, broke taboos, confounded expectations, and challenged the accepted wisdom and 'common sense' ideas of his day – and although his death on the cross seemed sudden and unexpected at the time, we can see that this was the natural climax of a life spent astounding others, serving others, and sacrificing himself for others.

Jesus presented a model of mission based on the power of attraction rather than compulsion, proximity rather than separation, love rather than fear, grace rather than guilt – and in the absence of his physical presence on earth our calling is to emulate him, to be his hands and feet in the world. Jesus himself said, 'As the Father has sent me, I am sending you' (John 20.21). Jesus was present in the everyday life of the people, and we too need to be part of this journey, travelling alongside people and speaking their language so they too may understand. We need to be right there in the thick of things; living lives that are deeply attractive, serving people wholeheartedly, meeting the needs of those around us, not ignoring those who might easily be overlooked, caring for people's mind, body and soul, seeing their lives changed for the better and, above all else, demonstrating the unconditional, everlasting, sacrificial love of Christ.

In all of this, I find it helpful to remind myself that when Jesus commissioned us to make disciples of all nations, he didn't just send us off with a smile and a wave to get on with it by ourselves. Instead, he followed this up with the assurance that he would always be with us – perpetually, consistently, and on every occasion (Matthew 28.20, AMP). This is one of those promises that never ceases to encourage me, because, to be honest, sometimes I still feel a little daunted by the task ahead. When this happens, I try to remember that as we follow Jesus' call to go into all the world, we are actually *following him* into the world. We are not taking him with us; he is already there, present and active, at work in all the people, places and situations we may come across. Not only that, but the Bible also suggests that when it comes to the crunch, we needn't worry about what to say or how to say it, because at that time the Holy Spirit will give us the right words to say (Matthew 10.18–20).

Although we have a great big part to play in God's purposes, we can rest assured that we aren't left to our own devices. This is God's mission, he's in charge, he determines the direction it takes, and at the end of the day it's God who brings people to faith, not us. Even Jesus said that he only did what he saw the Father doing (John 5.19), so how much more must we look to God to find out what he's doing, before we discern what to do ourselves? It may well be that God is doing things that we would never have guessed, moving in ways and in places that we would never have expected.

For me, the idea of joining in with something so much bigger than ourselves – beyond our ability to understand or quantify, throughout the world, throughout history, bigger than we can ever conceive – is both truly humbling and unbelievably exciting. When we follow God's lead, as likely as not he'll take us into places we would never have imagined, out of our comfort zones and into the fire.

2
Salt and Light

JON OLIVER

My mum won't be too pleased to find out like this, but I first went clubbing when I was still too young to get in – sneaking my way past the watchful eye of the bouncers with the help of a dodgy fake ID and a few older-looking school friends. To a certain extent this was initially just to see what all the fuss was about, but in no time at all the heady lure of getting wasted and pulling girls proved more than a match for my underdeveloped teenage willpower, and nights out on the town soon became a central purpose in my life.

Unfortunately, my faith had taken a backseat around this time, and for a while I experimented with a number of activities not particularly conducive to a healthy Christian lifestyle. But my love of clubbing was not all about such unsavoury aspects of club culture – for me, as for so many others, it was also about the music, the atmosphere, the letting loose, and the very real sense of togetherness, of a shared experience and understanding. Within the nightlife, friendships were formed, identity was explored, and small communities of regulars were developed. Often a night out would last far longer than the pubs and clubs stayed open – sometimes we'd crash back to someone's house, sometimes we'd stay up through the night with people we'd only just met, sometimes we'd watch the dawn rise while sharing stories and contemplating the meaning of existence.

Eventually, following a sudden and surprising revelation from

God, I decided to firm up my commitment as a Christian and began to re-evaluate my approach to life and faith – and to clubbing. I know some people who chose to step out of club culture completely once they'd found faith, who felt they needed to cut off all ties to their former lifestyle, to draw a line under the past. But not me. I still loved the social aspects of going out, and I still loved tearing it up on the dancefloor. Perhaps most importantly, this was where my friends were – and not just my friends, but also the thousands of others who go clubbing every week with the vague hope of finding some meaning, though all too often finding the gutter instead. Having spent so long misbehaving in the nightlife, it was tough figuring out how to live an authentic Christ-filled life in a context where I was used to acting so differently – but I knew I had to, because I know I couldn't just abandon this culture and these people I loved.

Third places

Since that time, this commitment to the social scene has been central to my understanding of mission – because for many people this is where real life is lived, where friendships are formed, meaning is sought, and informal communities are shaped. We live in an increasingly fragmented and dislocated society, where many don't know their next-door neighbours, and where work is often seen as a necessary evil rather than a meaningful vocation. Against this backdrop, people increasingly shape their identity through what they consume and how they spend their leisure time, and find their sense of belonging within informal gathering places such as cafés, coffee shops, gyms, galleries, shopping malls, internet cafés, social groups, sports clubs, community centres, pubs, clubs, bars, or wherever else people gather together. These are places where they can relax and be themselves, kick back or let their hair down, catch up with old friends or make new ones; where they can socialize, connect and feel part of a distinctive social community. These places are sometimes called 'third places'.[8]

Michael Frost writes, 'our first place is the home and the people with whom we live. Our second place is the workplace, the place where we spend most of our waking life. But the third places in our society are the bedrock of community life and all the benefits that come from such interaction.'[9] He suggests that our homes are increasingly seen as refuges of closely guarded privacy and that, despite the possibility of friendships being formed within the workplace, conversations at work are often kept purely functional, sometimes casually affable, but on the whole fairly guarded. In contrast to this, he says, 'It's in the third place that we let those guards down. It's here that we allow people to know us more fully. It's here that people are more willing to discuss the core issues of life, death, faith, meaning, and purpose.'[10]

This is not to suggest that mission cannot occur at home or in the workplace. Far from it. God is at work in the whole world, and we can engage with his mission wherever we find ourselves. But if we want to engage people in the big questions about the meaning of life and the possibility of God, the most effective context is likely to be those places where people feel free to be themselves, where they are already predisposed to meaningful conversation and open to contemplating new ideas. These are the very places where Jesus could regularly be found during his ministry – the Gospels are full of examples of such informal gathering places. As Michael Frost says, 'In a society where every third-place experience revolves around food . . . Jesus finds himself at the center of a place where people feel free to, well, just be! I would argue that in today's society, any attempt to model your life on the life of Christ must include a genuine attempt to hang out regularly in third places.'[11]

Following my recommitment to faith, I knew I still wanted to hang out in club culture – partly because I loved it, and partly because I was desperate to see the lives of my friends, and the culture I loved, transformed by Christ. It seems to me that if we're serious about reaching this generation (those in their late-teens, twenties and thirties), we need to make a genuine attempt to come alongside them on their territory – and one of the places we're most likely to find them is within the nightlife. A recent study by Mintel, a leading market research firm, found that around 73 per cent of 18–24-year-olds regularly attend late-night bars and clubs,[12] and just a few years ago the Home Office published estimates that annual admissions to

British nightclubs were around 200 million.[13] This contrasts starkly with estimates that only around 6 per cent of people in this age group regularly attend church in the UK.[14] So, if we're looking to engage with this generation, the nightlife might be a pretty good place to start – and for those of us already at home within club culture, it seems a pretty good idea to stay.

Night vision

As I hit my twenties, I moved to work for a church on the south coast, and was pleased to meet a number of other Christians who also enjoyed clubbing, and was delighted to discover that many of them were committed to finding a meaningful expression of their faith within this culture – and it was in this fledgling community that I really began to explore God's mission in club culture. As I got to know more people in the club scene, I was surprised to find out just how many Christians were involved – there were Christian DJs and musicians, bouncers and bar-staff, promoters, and those with their own bars. Then there were those involved in the nightlife in other ways – in the emergency services, various social services, working with prostitutes and homeless people, and those who wandered the streets at night offering care and prayer. But mostly it was simply clubbers – people who loved getting into the mix and partying all night.

Fast-forward a few more years, and I am now chaplain to the nightclubs in Bournemouth, and although I am still regularly pleased to meet other Christians involved in the club scene, I'm aware there are still relatively few of us. As Jesus said, 'The harvest is plentiful but the workers are few' (Matthew 9.37). This seems mainly due to the feeling in some parts of the church that clubbing isn't particularly appropriate for Christians. Given the widely pub-licized image of clubs as places of excessive drinking, drug-taking, sexual promiscuity and mindless violence, many seem to believe it best that Christians steer clear. Caution in these matters is reason-able, but sometimes what starts as justifiable concern can end up going too far. I've heard real horror stories about Christians facing serious condemnation for going clubbing, and I've heard of some being criticized for going into clubs even with overtly evangelistic intentions. A few years ago, when the Church of England licensed a Church Army evangelist as their first nightclub chaplain, the head of a noted Christian organization was quoted in the national press: 'I just find it so unbelievable as to be horrendous. The Church is once again playing to the gallery and behaving in an utterly absurd way.'[15]

Absurd?

From its very beginning, the church has been rooted in mission, in going into *all* the world; into the most beautiful and wonderful places, but also into the ugliest and most dismal; not avoiding the murky underbelly of society, but instead diving right in and trying to make a difference. So even if club culture is the proverbial den of iniquity (although many would disagree with that), then surely that's all the more reason for Christians to be there. John Stott says, 'When society goes bad, we Christians tend to throw up our hands in pious horror and reproach the non-Christian world; but should we not rather reproach ourselves? One can hardly blame unsalted meat for going bad. It cannot do anything else. The real question to ask is: where is the salt?'[16]

This is what Jesus said: 'You are the salt of the earth. But if the salt loses its saltiness, how can it be made salty again? It is no longer good for anything, except to be thrown out and trampled underfoot. You are the light of the world. A city on a hill cannot be hidden. Neither do people light a lamp and put it under a bowl. Instead they put it on its stand, and it gives light to everyone in the house' (Matthew 5.13–15).

So what does it mean to be the salt and the light? Light seems fairly obvious; it's essential to life, it heralds the day, gives us energy and casts away the darkness. We need to let our light shine out. Even a small lamp can illuminate a whole room, so the more lights we have and the brighter they shine, the fewer shadows there will be. Salt is more tricky, though, as it has countless different uses, some good, some bad. Most commonly we understand it in terms of its seasoning, preserving and purifying properties – but what use is it if kept stored away out of harm's way, tantalizingly close yet never touched, sprinkled or put to good use? Who keeps their salt-shakers under lock and key? Who keeps their lamps safely hidden under a bowl?

Get stuck in

St Paul once pointed out that when we say Jesus ascended on high, this means that he first came down to the lower parts of the earth (Ephesians 4.8–9, AMP). When Jesus came into the world, he didn't steer clear of the sinners or outcasts, or places considered unholy. Instead he got stuck into the midst of life in all its grimy reality. So, it seems clear that, if we want to emulate Jesus, we too need to get right into the thick of things, not ignoring the darkest corners or unsaltiest messes. Even if club culture is all that bad, this serves to give us still more of a biblical mandate to be there. It's not the healthy who need a doctor, but the sick; Jesus didn't come to call the righteous, but sinners (Matthew 9.10–13). So when I am asked whether I think it's appropriate for Christians to be involved in club culture, my answer is simple:

Yes!

An unequivocal Yes!

A great big fat YES at the top of my voice!

Yes! Yes! Yes! Yes! Yes!

Just as Peter and Paul had to trust God as he unexpectedly led them to engage with the Centurion and the Athenians (Acts 10, Acts 17.16ff), we too must be prepared to follow God wherever he leads us. There is nowhere we can go without the assurance that Jesus goes before us. That said, its understandable why some people are wary of club culture, especially as it's often younger (and potentially more impressionable) Christians who go clubbing. It's legitimate to show caution; in fact we would be remiss not to – the lure of sin can seem terribly attractive at times, and there are all manner of temptations within club culture. The prevalence of provocatively dressed and scantily clad bodies, for example, can present considerable temptation for anyone working or playing in nightclubs. However, I don't suppose this is any more so than for nineteenth-century missionaries faced with a multitude of girls dancing topless among the African tribes, and I suspect even the disciples had to deal with some personal discomfort witnessing 'a certain immoral woman' kissing Jesus' feet and washing them with her tears (Luke 7.36ff, NLT).

Facing temptation

I'll be straight with you, there are times when anyone involved in club culture will face temptation. Of course. But this is the case in any sphere of contemporary life. We live in an imperfect world, and temptation can be found all around, on television, on billboards, on the internet, on the street, at the beach, at the gym, at work, even at church! St Paul hinted at this when he said that in order not to associate with immoral people we would have to leave this world altogether (1 Corinthians 5.9–10)!

Let's not be naïve, though. If you have a particular struggle – say, with drugs, alcohol or overt sexuality – then maybe a nightclub isn't the most sensible place in which to be. It makes sense to stay away, at least until you feel strong enough to overcome the temptation. The important thing, though, is finding a way to overcome it. Avoidance isn't a lasting strategy. If we're going to face temptation every which way we turn, we need to face our fears at some point. Ant Newman (Chapter 4) has this to say on the subject:

> Discipleship is the key. I strongly believe that this is discipleship; not how to operate within a Christian gathering, but how to live a Christ-filled life in the real world. If we can't disciple people to deal with their sexuality, their weaknesses, alcohol, peer pressure, and so on, then are we actually discipling them at all? We have to face our fears – and that's the problem isn't it, fear? I believe that if we are to let each other and the Holy Spirit disciple us, then we have to walk boldly into the unknown, into temptation, into our fears – and guess what, learn to overcome them, and overcome ourselves. We can't hide from God, and we can't hide from ourselves. (Remember in the Garden of Eden, when Adam tried to

hide?) I think that often we try to limit where others should go not because we fear for them, but because we project our own weaknesses and fears on to them – maybe because we never dealt with them ourselves.

In the world, but not of it

Ant hit the nail on the head when he suggested we have to trust the Holy Spirit to disciple us and guide us into the world. How can we do any good unless we're right in there among it all? On the other hand, if we are going to make our lives among the people who inhabit the club scene, we need to be careful not to merge so seamlessly with the culture as to become indistinguishable from it. We must ensure we do not adopt those elements that contradict the gospel – after all, the Bible warns us not to let the world squeeze us into its mould (Romans 12.2, JBP). I have found the best way to ensure this is to make sure that my life is firmly rooted in a supportive Christian community, through which I can find the encouragement and accountability I need to continue working in this environment without selling out, and to continue serving in the long term without burning out.

As Christians, we are chosen out of the world (John 15.19), but unless we're going to try to leave the planet altogether, or go off and live in isolated communities as the Amish do, then surely we have to accept that we are not so much called out of the world, as called out from *the ways of the world*. We are called both to be true to our cultural context, and to be counter-cultural in our lifestyle. But how exactly are we supposed to be different? We are called to be a holy people, but Jesus makes it clear that holiness is not about the places we go; rather, it's about what we *do* when we get there – that it's not so much about what's on the outside, but what's going on inside that counts (Matthew 23.25–27). Tony Campolo suggests that somehow we have 'defined a Christian as someone more pious than the rest of the world. What did people say about Jesus? They didn't call him pious! He had a lousy testimony . . . They called him a winebibber, glutton, someone who hangs around with whores and publicans. Jesus was too busy expressing compassion to measure up to the expectations of piety. And I think we need to be more Christ-like.'[17]

Once in a while wouldn't it be nice if, like Jesus, we stood out not just for the naughty things we don't do, but for the good things we *do* do?

So where do we draw the line? We all have our own boundaries, but when we look to Jesus we find that he seemed to take deliberate pleasure in crossing the boundaries of the religious elite, those who considered themselves more pious than the rest. So when we start to draw up our own boundaries, who's to say that Jesus won't come along and trample all over them? God is who he is, and will go where he will go. We simply follow along in his wake. We need have no fear. As St Paul said, 'If God is for us, who can be against us?' (Romans 8.31).

The more we withdraw from the world around us, the less able we are to fulfil the command of Jesus to go into all the world and make disciples of all nations (Matthew 28.18–19). And this is the Great Commission after all – Jesus' parting words. You've got to assume it was fairly important.

God is at work in the world, and although we should show wisdom, seek accountability, and take precaution to avoid conforming to the ways of the world, we mustn't let fear stop us from getting right in there with him. We have to trust in the Holy Spirit to guide and protect us. Wherever we go, we can be certain that Jesus has already gone ahead of us – guiding us, leading us, beckoning us to join him in his mission. When Mike Riddell says that God's mission is like an open river that flows where it will, he also suggests that this means we must accept that we cannot control its course or its depth.[18] Instead we must look to God to show us where to swim. In responding to God's call, we may need to leave behind the safety of the riverbank, to go beyond our securities and certainties, and into the unknown – relying only on his guiding hand. As Jesus taught, and history shows, God will not be confined by our boundaries or restricted by our expectations.

3
Spirituality of the Age

JON OLIVER

When we think about club culture, it's all too easy to focus entirely on the naughty and depressing bits – the excessive drinking, drugs, violence, random sexual encounters, the relentless hedonistic pursuit of self-gratification. But this isn't all club culture has to offer. There are also the beautiful and uplifting bits – the music, creativity, dancing, friendships, the joyful celebration of simply being alive. Our task is not just to avoid and censure the negative aspects of club culture, but to affirm and encourage the positive elements, those wonderful things that the Bible heartily extols. As Pete Greig says, 'We aim to find the traces of God's goodness in every culture and enjoy these graces to the full. We're not there to condemn the place but to celebrate the life and love of God in it. One aspect of bringing redemption, we believe, is to magnify all that is wonderful about the world.'[19]

This is not to suggest that the gospel cannot critique culture – there will be aspects of any culture that are irreconcilable with Christianity, and there are certainly aspects of club culture that stand contrary to faith. However, there are also elements that can provide a suitable home for the gospel, and it is through locating these that we are able to offer the hope of the good news to people from within their own framework of understanding. As John Mbiti suggests, 'The gospel does not throw out culture – instead it settles in the culture and makes its impact on the lives of the people within that culture . . . The gospel does not *reject* culture, but *transforms* it.'[20] This is how the gospel has found its home in almost every nation, tribe and tongue throughout the world, and this is at the very core of our call to be the salt and the light. As Eugene Peterson phrases Jesus' words so wonderfully in *The Message*: 'Let me tell you why you are here. You're here to be salt-seasoning that brings out the God-flavours of this earth . . . Here's another way to put it: You're here to be light, bringing out the God-colours in the world' (Matthew 5.13–14, MSG).

Wherever there is love, there is something of God present. Wherever there is creativity, we can see a hint of God's handiwork. Wherever there is community, we can hear an echo of God's perfect community in the Trinity. Wherever there is music, dance, celebration and joy, we can taste the God-flavours of the world. Wherever there is beauty, we can see God made visible. As St Paul said, 'since the creation of the world God's invisible qualities – his eternal power and divine nature – have been clearly seen, being understood from what has been made, so that people are without excuse' (Romans 1.20). This doesn't mean God is revealed only in the trees and flowers and all the pretty things, but that he can be seen in and through *all* of his creation.

We don't put salt on our food because of its taste, but to enhance the wonderful flavours already there. Likewise, Jesus' call for us to be the salt of the earth suggests we need to bring out the 'God-flavours' already within club culture. Although these hints of God may not have found their expression in the way God intended, they nevertheless have the fingerprints of God upon them. Our task is to bring out the good bits, draw out the positives, highlight the places where God is already at work in all the situations we come across – and in this way to point towards the source of this grace and goodness. God is active in the whole world, moving towards people and drawing them towards him, inspiring them to search him out. As St Paul explained, 'His purpose was for the nations to seek after God and perhaps feel their way toward him and find him – though he is not far from any one of us. For in him we live and move and exist' (Acts 17.27–28, NLT). One area where this is particularly evident is in the spirituality that can sometimes be found within club culture.

Clubbing spirituality

For almost as long as clubbing has been around, there's been widespread interest in exploring and analysing the spiritual dimensions of the clubbing experience. It seems little wonder, since club culture is awash with religious symbolism, from the names of clubs or nights – such as Heaven, Eden and Godskitchen – to the frequent use of spiritually evocative lyrics and gospel samples in major club anthems, and the Christian iconography commonly incorporated into club décor, publicity and visuals. And then of course there's the transcendent, euphoric and numinous experiences often reported among clubbers.

I remember the night several years ago when I first noticed the similarities between a big, concert-style, youth worship meeting, and the dancefloor of a cavernous club. As I looked out over the sea of people coming together in the moment, I could see countless arms lifted, bodies moving, eyes gleaming, lungs bursting, hearts longing for something more. Of course, the similarities only went so far, but nevertheless my eyes began to be opened to the plausibility of there being a spiritual dimension to the clubbing experience. Over time, I became convinced that many clubs were full of people trying to find an experience to take them beyond the daily grind. And for many Christian clubbers, this is precisely what they do find. A friend of mine once said that some of the most amazing and intimate moments she's spent with God have been in nightclubs. It could be argued that this says more about her experiences of church than about the spiritual character of clubbing, but – when coupled with similar testimonies from other Christian clubbers – it certainly points towards the fact that it's possible to encounter God on the dancefloor.

However, it's not only Christians who report out-of-the-ordinary experiences within the nightlife. Many people find that the various elements of clubbing – the charged atmosphere, brooding darkness, pulsing lights, chemical stimulants, energy expended, the throbbing beats and rhythmic patterns of the music, and the fluctuation between moments of deeply personal introversion and those of complete engagement with fellow dancers – can combine to create an incredibly intense experience. For many this leads to sensations of euphoria, ecstasy, interconnectedness, escape and transcendence.[21] Some commentators have even drawn parallels between the spiritual experiences occurring in clubs, and those usually associated with churches – suggesting that as people continue to disengage from traditional religious institutions, nightclubs have become a contemporary alternative for meeting the 'religious' impulse. As Gordon Lynch says, 'the mainstream post-rave dance scene is a "secondary institution" supporting the new social form of religion'.[22]

I sometimes wonder, though, whether this is evidence of a 'clubbing spirituality' or simply indicative of the wider interest in spirituality burgeoning within Western culture. After all, the whole of our society is awash with books and films rooted in the supernatural, with music and fashion containing suggestions of spirituality, and with people increasingly turning to guardian angels, spirit guides, faith healers, or even outer space in their search for meaning. John Drane says, 'To traditional Christians, this might be unfamiliar territory. But it certainly means that these people are spiritually open as no other generation within living memory.'[23] There seems to be a growing consensus that Western society underwent something of a spiritual revolution near the end of the twentieth century, and that we are still witnessing a surging interest in spirituality – in that which goes beyond the self, in the unexplained, in the possibility of a superior being.

When I first started looking into this subject, I read all sorts of books and articles, went on various courses, and had innumerable conversations with people involved in engaging with the spirituality of our times. I became convinced that people everywhere were asking great, searching questions of themselves and of the world, and I became incredibly excited about the opportunities this presented for exploring with people the good news of Jesus. But then I started my current job, moved from simply thinking about mission and spirituality and got stuck into the real thing – and to begin with, I found little evidence to support these claims about a burgeoning spirituality. I'd expected to find a generation of spiritual searchers on a quest for real and transformative meaning, but on the whole I found most people were simply looking for a good time. I soon began to wonder whether all this talk about contemporary spirituality was just wishful thinking on the part of Christians eager to find points of connection with culture.

Buried spirituality

However, as I spent more time in the nightlife, got to know more people, and became more rooted in the culture, I realized that there were in fact countless people interested in spirituality – but that in many, if not most cases, it was hidden away. All too often these thoughts, questions and longings seemed to be buried beneath people's inability to articulate their thoughts or fear of being ridiculed, beneath past hurts or disappointments, beneath a mass of confusion and doubt, or beneath the hectic hubbub and stifling stress of the daily grind. In fact, I have met relatively few who are engaged in an active spiritual 'search' or 'quest'. Instead I have found that while many are interested in spirituality, they're not usually preoccupied with it. In other words, people of this generation may be asking the big questions, but they're not necessarily actively searching out the answers. They may be willing to engage with spiritual matters when opportunities arise, but most are not going out of their way to seek out these opportunities. As Phil Rankin says, 'it is very obvious that young people are asking spiritual questions and that they have a desire to reflect on their spirituality. There is also clear evidence that many young people are having extraordinary experiences that they do not fully understand but they have a desire to reflect on . . . But this awareness is often buried within the demands of everyday life.'[24]

Nevertheless, I have found that given the right circumstances and opportunities, most people will readily engage in explorations of spirituality, and that, with the appropriate prompting, will leap at the chance to unpack and explain their understanding of the big questions about life and God. Within this they will often show a real, and sometimes surprising, interest in exploring and unpacking our understanding of life, faith and God in turn. A recent study of young people and clubbers (aged 14–25) found that the majority interviewed were genuinely interested in spiritual matters, and were usually eager to discuss and explore their spirituality when the opportunity was offered. In concluding the report, Phil Rankin says, 'They want to consider [spiritual questions] so that they might better know what they believe and can connect this belief to life. But the space and opportunity to reflect is not being adequately provided . . . It is essential that the correct space is provided to enable them to fully consider the spiritual questions and to connect to that which is currently "buried".'[25]

If people are willing to engage with spirituality when given the space, surely our response must involve a genuine attempt to help discover and create appropriate opportunities for them to do so. They're unlikely to come knocking down the doors of our churches looking for such opportunities, so we need to go to them and journey with them, creating space along the way to ask the big questions alongside one another. Whether this is through informal conversations, long-term friendships, or spaces created specifically to facilitate spiritual exploration, the underlying principle remains the same – we need to make ourselves accessible to those who would never dream of turning to the church for guidance or companionship in their life journeys. If this spirituality is buried away under the surface ready to be uncovered when the opportunities arise, it is possible that this may occur without our help. So the questions we have to ask ourselves are: Do we want to be there when it happens? And, if so, is there anything we can do to encourage or enable this?

Questions of the heart

Of course, this isn't the full picture. Though I have come across a small handful of people actively engaged in a meaningful spiritual search, and countless others whose spirituality is hidden, I have also met vast numbers who seemingly have no interest at all in the possibility of God. These are people who are likely to dismiss out of hand the suggestion that there is anything beyond the material world, convinced that there is nothing more than those things we can see, hear, touch, taste, buy, use, consume, and throw away. In my experience, these people seem comfortable with the limitations this worldview entails, showing scant interest in finding any deeper meaning – they mainly just want to be happy and have a good time.

This echoes the findings of another recent study that looked at the worldviews of those aged 15–25. It found that most people were seemingly content with the idea of a life without God – not overly concerned with finding something to fill the 'God-shaped hole' within, nor with finding an overarching 'meta-narrative' to give meaning to everyday life. Instead, their primary concern seemed to be finding happiness for themselves, along with their friends and family, in the here and now. Sara Savage suggests that the prevailing worldview among those interviewed was that, 'This world, and all life in it, is meaningful *as it is* . . . In other words, there is no need to posit ultimate significance elsewhere beyond the immediate experiences of everyday life.'[26]

For years I struggled to formulate an appropriate response to this worldview, then suddenly it hit me – we're never going to be able to find a 'one-size-fits-all' response to the incredible variety of people and situations we come across. It is simply something we need to thrash out as we go along. Sometimes it may become clear that the people we meet have rejected the idea of God due to a misguided notion of Christianity – and perhaps we may need to be committed to understanding and dispelling these misconceptions before we can begin exploring further. Some may have rejected the possibility of faith on the basis of very real hurt suffered at the hands of the church – and perhaps we need to be prepared to offer a sincere apology before we can point with hope towards our loving Father who has plans to prosper us and not to harm us (Jeremiah 29.11). With others, there may be contradictions between what they claim to believe and what their actions reveal – and perhaps we need to challenge these contradictions and to sensitively provoke them to question the assumptions they've made in forming their conception of the universe, and of their place in it.

Perhaps. Perhaps. *Perhaps.*

There are no hard and fast rules. There are no easy answers, and any attempt to offer them is likely to end up sounding glib, shallow or meaningless. To a certain extent, I think we've fallen at the first hurdle if we try to find straightforward answers to the complexity of human existence. There are no magic methods or secrets for success. The only strategy is love. Sometimes it's only our love, and God's love working through us, that can break through these barriers of pain, doubt, disbelief or confusion; and sometimes it's only by truly walking alongside people that we can build the trust and openness needed even to begin this process. While this *can* occur within the context of a fleeting interaction, more often than not it will require us to invest in real, loving, long-term relationships. Sometimes it can take months, even years, before people start to feel able to open up, before they really feel it's safe to explore and to ask questions.

The best starting place is often simply to listen. Unless we are willing to truly listen – to people's doubts and fears, to the pain they have suffered and the problems they're facing, to the ideas they hold and their understanding of the world – we are unlikely to be able to respond effectively, and instead are likely to end up offering unwanted answers to unasked questions. So many seem to have given up asking questions, simply because they've been left unanswered for so long. Perhaps we need to start by taking these people's concerns more seriously, and by truly listening to their questions before we try to seek answers together. Perhaps we need to understand ourselves as fellow pilgrims on a journey – travelling alongside people, listening to their stories, sharing our own, and witnessing to the love and truth we have experienced ourselves in Christ. As Jesus said, 'be generous with your lives. By opening up to others, you'll prompt people to open up with God, this generous Father in heaven' (Matthew 5.16, MSG).

But what about those people who simply don't care? For many, these questions aren't even on their radar – they seem to have genuinely never given a moment's thought to the possibility that there might be anything beyond the material world. Perhaps we need to challenge them to consider the possibility that there is more to life than the here and now. Perhaps we need simply to take our time, patiently sowing seeds of love and truth into their lives. Perhaps we need to attempt to awaken within people that which Ann Morisy calls 'the capacity to be astonished and to be surprised by the more in life'.[27] We may not be able to overturn this materialistic world-view overnight, but by allowing people to witness the presence of God in our own lives, we may be able to whet their appetites and sow seeds of intrigue – we may be able to encourage people to consider, even for a moment, the possibility of God.

Graham Cray says: 'The further we travel beyond those with any sort of contact with the Church, the further back we will have to start. We live in an instant culture, which cannot be reached by instant missionary tactics. There is no alternative to what we have called prior mission . . . this will involve starting where young people are, rather than where we would like them to be, and helping them to articulate their own questions, rather than expecting them to respond to ours.'[28] He suggests that this will entail meeting people on their territory, establishing the maximum common ground, offering resources for coping with life, being willing to walk alongside people as they explore and, above all, investing in real, long-term relationships. He also says this 'will involve positive action to benefit them, regardless of their immediate responsiveness to the Christian message'.[29]

Seeking to benefit others

A few years ago, I heard a talk about the 'ethics of conversion', in which we were asked this question: 'Would we continue to love, serve and seek to benefit someone, even if we knew they would never become a Christian?' As we mulled over the implications of this challenge, it occurred to me that if the love we offer is to be truly unconditional, we can't put restrictions on our love and service.

If we truly believe the good news, if we wholeheartedly trust that God's love is unconditional, we need to allow this truth to permeate our entire beings. We need to take Jesus at his word when he says that we are to love one another as he has loved us, with all-consuming, everlasting, unconditional love (John 13.34). We need to strive with all our heart, mind, soul and strength to love our neighbours as ourselves: to offer help to the helpless, give hope to the hopeless, comfort the discomfited, love the unlovable, care for the careless, see the captives set free, and send forth as delivered the oppressed and the downtrodden, the broken and the bruised, the burdened and the battered.[30]

We need to love our neighbour not just so they ask us why we're being so nice, but because Jesus told us to – because loving our neighbour as ourselves is our response to the love that we have been given in him.

We need to identify the needs of those around us, and follow God's lead in developing an appropriate and sensitive response to these needs. We live in one of the most materially rich countries in the world, yet our society is full of people in need; not just people with material needs, but also those with deep-rooted personal, social and emotional needs; and not just people with obvious needs, but those who seem to have it all, who may not even recognize their need. Surely we need to seek to benefit these people too, striving to see their lives enriched, enhanced and changed for the better, regardless of their responsiveness to the Christian message.

If we offer our love and service on the sole basis that we get an opportunity to talk to people about Jesus, I sometimes wonder whether we are actually serving our own agenda rather than truly serving *them*. Yet these are precisely the opportunities I long for – to come alongside people, to encourage them in their spiritual explorations, and to offer an explanation for the hope I have in Jesus. And I strive towards these opportunities with great excitement and expectation because, if mission is God's movement towards humanity, my response has to be to encourage people to move towards him in turn. This might mean drawing out the God-flavours and God-colours in people's lives, or pointing out the fingerprints of God in the world around us. This might mean demonstrating Jesus' unconditional love, or encouraging people to entertain the possibility of God. This might mean holding their hand as they take a tentative step towards him, or cheering them on as they take a giant leap of faith into a relationship with Christ.

However, this might not mean any of these things. We may never see these people become Christians and, even if we do, it could be months, years, or even a whole lifetime before this happens. Meanwhile, I am convinced that we need to try our best to serve these people with all that we are, to love them as Christ first loved us, and to be prepared to offer an explanation for the hope we have – regardless of whether we ever see them respond to the message of hope we carry.

4
Freedom Funk

ANT NEWMAN (SOUTHAMPTON)

I became a Christian within the space of two toilet cubicle visits. The first was at Club UK in Wandsworth, south London, while Carl Cox was DJing in the main room. The second was in my grotty student accommodation a few months later.

A few years before these spiritual lavatory encounters, my mum and my sister became Christians and managed to persuade me along to a couple of church meetings – which were full of awful music, bad clothes, and people with beards. Nevertheless, it was clear that God was hanging out with them – I could really feel his presence and love. It was amazing, but it totally messed with my hedonistic worldview of 'Do whatever you want as long as you don't hurt anyone else' (which was ridiculous really, because whatever you do, or don't do, inevitably affects other people in some way). My mum and my sister started praying for me, and got their new church friends to pray for me too . . . my unbelieving days were numbered!

Back to Club UK – with the usual 'Final Frontier' Friday-night hard techno bash heating up in the main room, I was talking to God inside a toilet cubicle out back. My prayer went something like this: 'God, I know you're real, but I can't get through this evening without taking this Ecstasy tablet, so I'm gonna take it, but please don't let me die if it's a dodgy pill.' As I prayed, I felt God clearly speak to me, and I knew it wasn't drug-induced voices. I'd taken Ecstasy plenty of times before and, although its effects can be powerful, never before had its chemically induced high included the conviction of how sin hurts God, others and myself, nor the sense of how superficial hedonism is, compared to the love and beauty of God. He cut straight through the effects of the drug and into the core of my being with sobering clarity.

My second divine toilet experience was some time later. Most of my mates were doing a spot of small-time drug-dealing, and within a short space of time two of them got sent to prison, a third fled the country to avoid being nicked, and a fourth suffered mental health problems and ended up being sectioned. At that time, my whole life revolved around partying, music, art and taking drugs. Most of my conversations were about drugs, and all my anecdotes were about times I'd been on drugs. Late one evening, I hid away in a shabby toilet cubicle and asked myself 'What is my life coming to?' God seemed to be listening, and turned up for a little chat – I suddenly felt his presence around me so strong, so euphoric, so pure, so real! For 20 minutes I had the breath of God sweep through my guts. I said sorry to him for my sins, and yes to his will for my life. I remember seeing a picture in my mind's eye of countless clubbers and ravers worshipping God, and I emerged from the toilet desperate for others just like me to know that Jesus Christ is very real, and that he loves them very much.

A natural high

Soon all my mates wanted to know why I'd quit drugs. I tried to explain how I'd met God, but they all just thought I'd taken too much acid and lost it! Eventually, though, they realized it was a genuine, long-term decision and not some passing religious fad. In fact, one of my mates made a bet with his girlfriend that I could last longer on the dancefloor because my inspiration was God. She was convinced that amphetamines (speed) would give her the edge, but my mate knew I could rave longer worshipping God. Bizarre, but true. Some people make the comparison between being into God and being into drugs – they recognize their need for something 'extra' to get them through life or give them more confidence and energy. People often use drugs as a substitute for God. That was certainly true with me.

Over the next few years I had many opportunities for God-conversations with friends, old and new, at various pubs, clubs and parties – it seemed the most natural thing to share my faith within that culture, and made perfect sense to me. These are the places where people hang out to relax and chat. Even before I became a Christian, I would stay up into the early hours talking about the meaning of life in places like these. I really wanted other Christians to understand that we could see God touch people's lives within club culture, but it felt like some church people just didn't get it. I tried encouraging other Christians to expect God to use them when they were out on the town, but most of them either didn't go out much, or got drunk when they did. As much as it frustrated me, I realized that I was trying too hard to make something happen with people who weren't into it.

Getting organized

A while later I moved to Southampton, where I was asked to DJ at a night promoting fair trade. As I was playing records and watching everyone on the dancefloor, I felt God say, 'I know all the people who come to these clubs, and their search for pleasure and fulfilment in drink, drugs, music, dancing, pulling and sex. I know all the bouncers, promoters, bar-staff, DJs, MCs and drug-dealers. I know all of their stories. I know what they are looking for in life. I'm just waiting for some people to be available for me to use them to minister to these people.'

This was the prompt I needed, so I began to gather some mates who felt similarly to meet and pray together. Before long we were regularly clubbing together, and meeting weekly just like any normal cell group might. As we began to spend time together, committing ourselves to particular clubs, and DJing certain nights, we began to get to know different people in the scene: DJs, promoters, MCs, musicians, regular punters and, interestingly enough, several people who'd strayed from church, but felt they could relate to us. One of our lads set up an email group, and we would send out weekly mailouts with all the information about the different club nights we would be going to, along with suggestions for things to pray about. At the time we really wanted to put on our own club night – especially as all our Christian contemporaries seemed to be running their own nights – but every time we prayed about it, it just felt wrong. In our hearts we knew that God wanted us to focus on friendships and community, rather than getting caught up in the politics of running a night. The local scene was already bursting with loads of small nights, so why faff about trying to compete with them, when we could support the nights of others and invest our time in connecting with people instead? After a while, I decided to cut my hours down at work and go part time, so I could plough more energy into serving and facilitating this community of people reaching into club culture. My new church let me use their office space, computers and phones, and eventually ended up helping me financially too. In everything I did, I was accountable to my church leaders, not because they requested it, but because I wanted to be answerable to those older and wiser than me – the last thing I wanted was to become a law unto myself.

Community stories

A few years down the line, and I now have the enormous privilege of being a part of what has become a vibrant community of Christians who are creatively and holistically involved in Southampton's social scene. One of these people has only recently become a Christian – he's really struggled with drugs, but is steadily growing into a great man of God. He is incredibly talented and could earn a tidy sum as a professional musician, but while he gets established in his faith he has chosen to work locally, while recording and gigging (and sharing his faith) with chart-topping artists on the side. This is just one of the many people now part of our community. We may have started off as a bunch of mates simply clubbing, praying and chatting to people about God, but we have ended up with something far more diverse, interesting and church-like than we ever expected. I'd like to introduce you to some of them.

Adi is a leather-wearing biker who uses hair straighteners, loves poetry and rock music, and is currently studying drama. He regularly hangs out at a creative open mic night at a local club, often participating in the myriad of weird and wonderful acts. He performs monologues, poems and film extracts, with a heavy provocative edge to challenge his audience. As he grew in confidence he began to perform controversial pieces such as the 'parable of the good paedophile', which took a despised member of society and asked whether they were capable of doing good. Pretty hardcore stuff, but that's the type of edgy crowd hanging out down there. We usually pray for him before he goes down to the club, and inevitably he finds opportunities for 'God chats' with some of the regular punters. He recently performed the classic 'Choose life' section from the film *Trainspotting*, and afterwards invited people on an Alpha course, which one guy signed up for. Adi has his struggles with God, church and depression, but he is seeking to find truth himself, serving Jesus in the way he knows how, and challenging others along the way – and that looks pretty good to me.

Purpose B (aka Matt) is a rehabilitation support worker during the day, and a hip-hop, funk, cosmic disco and breaks DJ during the night. Shortly after he moved to Southampton, Matt and I prayed that God would give us DJ residencies together, and lo! before long we started DJing at the same club – Matt playing hip-hop in one room and me playing drum & bass in another. I guess for me it's the 'strength in numbers' philosophy – after all, Jesus sent out the disciples in twos (Mark 6.7). Both of us began to make new friends at the club and had some really interesting conversations about God, particularly with the promoter and the host MC, who regularly grills Matt about God when they go for a pint together. When his family went through a hard time recently, I offered to pray with him but he said that although he'd really like to pray, he didn't know how. I explained that the best way to learn is by doing, and we agreed to meet up and pray. He took to it like a duck to water, and ended up praying for his family situation, our friends, and even for me. He's still wrestling with the idea of God, but we reckon it's only a matter of time before he finds Jesus. As Matt continues to progress as a DJ, he feels that most, if not all, the connections he's made have been God-engineered. He has loads of stories about bumping into promoters in the street, with opportunities and invitations to DJ simply opening up. He's DJed in pretty much every decent venue in the city, supporting many world-famous acts, and has had countless opportunities to share his faith with DJs, clubbers, promoters and bar-staff. I've seen Matt boldly face the challenges and temptations thrown up by loving and walking alongside these 24-hour party people – and of course he's had to face the usual barrage of jokes that poke fun at the fact that he's chosen not to sleep around, but places his value on marriage instead.

Graham is a playwright, general creative and college lecturer, who currently enjoys writing and performing plays in clubs and festivals – employing a deadly combination of comedy, philosophy, spirituality and existentialism. We first met at my church, when he had just returned from an eight-year vacation from all things 'church'. We struck up a conversation, and it turned out that he'd been promoting and partying in Prague and the Isle of Wight for the last few years (to the eventual detriment of his mental health and general well-being). We began to go for nights out on the Isle of Wight together, and before long we started hosting a monthly drum & bass night in Newport. I'd bring some Christian mates, Graham would hook up with his old party buddies, and when our night finished we'd all go on to another club together – and more often than not something interesting would crop up. One night in particular we had an amazing time; one of Graham's friends (who had a habit of taking lots of drugs and drinking very heavily) was in a right old state, hanging on to the DJ booth while I was DJing and pretending to have sex and whipping himself. On the outside he was a hardcore party animal, but on the inside he was losing the plot. That night, Graham had a real heart-to-heart with him, explaining about Jesus bringing light into the darkness and madness that his friend so often felt. It was a very tender and desperate moment. Later that evening, I was chatting with another of Graham's friends, when she began to really open up. It turned out that she'd had an abortion, and felt a great deal of guilt and shame about it – she knew I was a Christian,

33

and I was able to share with her about God's forgiveness. Later, as we set off home, we came across a girl passed out in the road. With her short skirt covering very little, she was totally vulnerable to someone taking advantage of her. I found a female friend and together we managed to bring her round, pick her up, and walk her home safely. The simple act of a couple of people making themselves available to God meant we were able to help this girl avoid a potentially disastrous situation. Praise God!

Amy & Rosie are two more Islanders. Although they have left the Isle of Wight, the Island hasn't left them. It seems to have that effect. They have been involved in setting up a venue called 'Solace' at Bestival and the Isle of Wight Festival. Solace is a creative chill-out tent where tea, coffee and masses of home-baked cakes (lovingly made by locals) are given out free to bleary-eyed festival-goers. There is a prayer-room at the back, and people often make prayer requests. It's an awesome force of kindness, and a real place of refuge – but they simply see it as their contribution to the festivals they enjoy. Amy says they love to celebrate and to join in with the creativity of the festivals, and that they simply want to demonstrate God's love, and show that he can be found throughout the festivals and in the creativity there. Sometimes I have had the privilege of DJing at Solace, and have witnessed first-hand the amazing opportunities the team have created to show God's kindness to people (Acts 28.2). Overall, it's been brilliant having the girls as part of our community.

Crispy & Rach. I first met Crispy when he leaned over the DJ booth in a local club, shook my hand, and blurted out 'Wicked tunes!' In no time we began to pray and scheme together about seeing God move in the clubs. God has given Crispy a Duracell battery more powerful than anyone else I know – when the tunes come on, Crispy lets loose and the dancefloor is decimated. An all-in-one boiler suit with a smiley face on the back, a luminous builder's waistcoat, white gloves and glow-sticks would be Crispy's daily get-up if his wife Rach would let him! Crispy has faithfully served and helped lead our community for the last few years, and his recent marriage to Rach has resulted in a dynamic duo – they have always had an open home to our community, cooking and caring for people throughout this time. Together with other rebels with a cause, headed up by SPEAK (a network of people campaigning and praying about issues of global injustice), they organized the 'Big Dress Festival', in which a bunch of local DJs, bands and other acts came together for a two-day festival in Southampton city centre to raise awareness around issues of justice. It was a real triumph, with loads of our community (believers and non-believers alike) serving together for the greater good. Church was pushed out into the local arena and our local MP even turned up to support it. Similar to Samson's hair, we suspect Crispy's power is within his beard!

Kat & Hannah are a couple of cheeky young lasses in our community. They felt God prompt them to start up a breakdance society at their university, and so 'Breakin ground' was formed. Having prayed that they would find the right venue, they spoke to the manager of a local bar and he said they could use his bar free every Monday night. Meanwhile, we discovered that another lad was running a breakin crew in his local Methodist church, through which he has seen countless God-given opportunities to share his faith with fellow breakers. Add to this yet one more breakin session in town, run by another local Christian lad, and it turns out that the three main breakin crews in Southampton are all run by Christians! God has yet again done his thing and we now have a great network of breakers in the city, representing Christ simply by being a part of this head-spinning community.

Jellybass (aka Joe and Chix) are a couple of DJs/producers from a nearby church who we've become friends with – we often pray together, encouraging one another to maintain accountability and integrity in the music scene. They have recently been signed to a record label, and big-name DJs are already playing their tunes – it's really exciting, but for them it's all for a higher purpose. They've recently become friends with another local DJ and his girlfriend. Although this DJ says he's happy being an atheist, and though his girlfriend walked away from church a long time ago, they both attend a home group run by the Jellybass boys. A few other friends they know through the local music scene who aren't Christians also come along to their home group. It's amazing. A few weeks ago we spent the whole evening talking about the delicate issue of feeling hurt, judged and misunderstood by churchgoers. One of the girls suddenly started crying, opening up about how hurt she felt, but explaining that through it all she still held on to the fact that God was real and he loved her. We all shared our stories of how we had found God, and later one of the DJs admitted that he was intrigued by people who seem to have found peace within themselves – something he's noticed in a lot of Christians. Isn't it wonderful when atheists, and those who've been hurt by the church in the past, not only find they are welcome in church, but that they also have a voice and a contribution to make?

The connection

These are just a few of the people I could introduce you to, but I'm running out of space, so I'll tell you a few more stories and be done with it. One night a few of us were in a local club, and after a good session breakin and messing about to the music, I got into a conversation with an older guy propping up the bar. We started off chatting about breakdancing, but ended up talking about the war on terror and that old chestnut – right-wing religious fundamentalism. (I can't begin to tell you how many people have wanted to discuss this topic in clubs and pubs up and down the country.) I shared with him my thoughts on this complex situation, and he became very interested when he found out that I was a Christian, but didn't necessarily hold the same views as the fundamentalists who all too often hog the media limelight. We began to discuss Jesus' teachings around peace, love and non-violence. He had obviously been racking his brain for some time about the whole 'God issue' and shared his thoughts with me. We finished our conversation, and I headed back to the dancefloor. However, before I left the club later that night, I made sure I found him to say goodbye. He thanked me and said, 'I really appreciate you giving me the time of day, you didn't have to. I hope you don't mind but I've got some more questions.' We ended up sitting for ages chatting about God, and praying together. He had clearly gone out to drink his sorrows away, but in reality he just needed to talk to someone – and it's sad that his first port of call was not a church, but rather a club. Thank God he ended up meeting some of the church in the club.

Another time, a friend and I were at a party thrown by the singer of a local band, when a lad came over and started chatting up my female friend. (His opening line was: 'I like your shoes.' What a classic!) During the conversation he discovered that she was a Christian, and a discussion about God ensued. I ended up getting involved, and as we shared about being able to have a personal relationship with Jesus, and about church being a loving community, his ears pricked up. 'Now that's what I'm interested in: the connection!' he said intently. We shared our stories of how we became Christians, while he listened carefully and asked many questions, insisting that this 'connection' with God and with people was precisely what he was searching for. It turned out that he'd spent three years living in a Hare Krishna community looking for just that. Before we left I said to him, 'If you're up for it, I reckon we should pray.' He said that he wasn't sure he was ready to 'convert', and I reassured him that we could simply pray that God would somehow let him know he was real. He was well up for this, so we all prayed together there and then. The following Sunday he came to church with us – and loved it! A couple of weeks later, I went along to a live music night he organized, and he introduced me to his friends, saying, 'Hey, everyone, this is one of the Christians I was telling you about!' After this blunt yet surprisingly well-received introduction, he pointed to a friend and said, 'He's a tarot card reader, you guys should have some interesting things to chat about. . .' We did!

Where are we now?

As I said, when we were starting out I felt it was right to take a part-time job, so that I could still pay the bills (just about!) while having enough time to get out and about at night, facilitate and care for our community, organize our weekly gatherings, DJ regularly, run breakin sessions, see people pastorally during the day, and have lie-ins if I had a span of late nights in a row. Building a mission-focused community takes time and effort, and if you're thinking about getting involved in this sort of thing, you need to be sure of what you are doing, as it could mean some serious lifestyle changes. You need to work out what you're willing to give – or give up. Most people fit it in with the rest of their lives, and go out maybe once or twice a week. Gauge your capacity. Work out how much you want to do this, and do as much or as little as you feel called to.

After three years I decided to return to full-time work, and take more of a back seat from leading the community, allowing other people to take things on. I felt it was important to encourage them to know they could make it their own, and not simply replicate what I had done. I'm a firm believer that the people define the vision, ministry and structure, rather than the other way round. I think that leadership is about finding out what God has placed deep within people, and releasing them to be who God has made them to be, rather than forcing then into an unnatural mould. Too often I've seen someone come up with an idea, and then try to make other people fit into it – but I think that sucks big time! Years ago, a friend of mine switched me on to a model of leadership based on Proverbs 20.5, 'The purposes of the human heart are deep waters, but those who have insight draw them out.' Our community may have started out with clubbers, but God has drawn in such diversity to our group – including people who aren't even into music or clubbing – and we have become so much richer as a result. It hasn't been an easy transition, but we continually evolve, and recently a new leader has emerged and very naturally gathered a community of fellow surfers and snowboarders to enjoy their favourite sports together, and to represent Christ at the same time.

These stories might sound problem-free, but there have been some tough times too. During this key period of seeing new leaders emerge, there was a lot of disruption and manipulation, and for a while it seemed that the whole community would be torn apart – a stark reminder that the devil will use any situation to mess things up. I am wary of super-spiritualizing things, but I have grown to understand the utmost importance of praying for people and of not being naïve when evil forces are at work: 'pray in the Spirit on all occasions with all kinds of prayers and requests. With this in mind, be alert and always keep on praying for all the Lord's people' (Ephesians 6.18). These tensions have been at play in the church since the time of Paul and Barnabas. As St Peter wrote, 'Be alert and of sober mind. Your enemy the devil prowls around like a roaring lion looking for someone to devour' (1 Peter 5.8). We have to face the reality of this challenge, but if we push on through and are motivated by love for God and for people, we are sure to see Jesus build his kingdom.

However, there have been times I've wondered whether this whole thing was my own silly idea. Had I just gone ahead with what I wanted to do, or had God really spoken to me? This feeling used to really hit hard on nights when we hadn't seen anything really 'spiritual' happen. A few years down the line, though, I can clearly see the fruit of our long-term presence in the club scene. Was I doubting myself, doubting God, or simply doubting my ability to hear him? I still don't know, but I do know the Bible tells us that God is our shepherd, we are his sheep, and we will know his voice – so when God speaks, we have to learn to trust him (John 10.1–18). It is the same story throughout the Bible: Abraham, Moses, Joseph, Peter, Paul and countless others had to learn to trust God's voice. And guess what? It paid off! Not necessarily straight away, but always in the long term. In fact, quite often things got worse before they got better – and Jesus said we will have trouble in this world (John 16.33). I remember when I was first starting out, I spoke to Roger Ellis (leader of Revelation Church in Chichester) who told me very matter of factly, 'Yeah, it usually takes around ten years to establish anything of worth.' I think this was the moment I truly realized what I was letting myself in for, but when you have a God-given vision, sometimes the only way to turn it into reality is to put in the time and hard work. Our 'now' generation may not favour such a prospect, but as Gerald Coates (founder of the Pioneer network of churches) once told me, 'We're in it for the long haul!'

If I'm honest with you, I don't really know what I'm doing. I'm simply trying to live for Jesus in a way that seems real to me. I'm more interested in giving things a go than in whether they work or not, and I think God is more interested in a willing heart than in whether you manage to build an all-singing, all-dancing ministry. I may have lots of stories about trying to represent Jesus in clubs and pubs, but that's my journey so far. What's yours? Is it your time to step up? When we look in the mirror, we see a child of God staring back, waiting to go into all nations and make disciples (Matthew 28.19). That 'nation' may be your local nightclub, golf club, bingo hall, football team, supermarket, or wherever God leads you. My story may be one focused on club culture, but that's where I became a Christian, and it's a culture I understand. Where has God put you? What people group has he put around you? They are the future church waiting for you to introduce them to Jesus.

5

The Rubiks Cube

DOUG ROSS (BRISTOL)

It all started at age fourteen, after hearing some of my classmates talking about going to a club at the weekend. Before then I had never even entertained the thought of trying to get into an over-18s night – but with a few days of bumfluff growth to boost my confidence, I borrowed some of my dad's aftershave, spiked my hair, put on a shirt, and we were ready to rumble. As we joined the queue for the club, my heart began to beat faster than ever before – we looked much younger than everyone else, but we desperately hoped that our fake IDs would work. Suddenly the bouncers waved us past, and we were in. With an enormous sound-system, flowing alcohol and girls with next to nothing on, partying in a nightclub was a major change from playing with my Transformer figures, and was an experience that scared me half to death. I loved it! But it was the start of a very slippery slope.

Church soon became something I did for my parents' sake. Most of my mates were part of the same church, and didn't approve of my new lifestyle, so I hung around with them less and less. What started as a one-off adventure soon became a weekly ritual. Every Friday and Saturday night I could be found in town – drinking, smoking, making trouble and experimenting with drugs. However, the main reason I fell in love with clubbing was the music, and I decided to save up and buy some turntables. I couldn't afford them by myself, so I went halves on a second-hand set of Pro 150s with a friend –

buying a deck each, and splitting the cost of a mixer. Not really knowing how to DJ, it became increasingly frustrating to see the DJs play week in week out and me not being able to do it properly. But still I lived for the weekend.

The summer of '96

A couple of years later, a few of my old church mates invited me along to Soul Survivor (a Christian youth festival). It didn't really appeal to me at the time, other than I hoped there would be lots of good-looking girls there. Little did I know that the week would turn my life upside down. I eventually agreed to go, and one evening the speaker invited everyone who wanted the ultimate buzz, a touch of the Holy Spirit, to come up to the front of the venue to be prayed for. To my amazement, my heart started to beat faster than it did that very first time I queued to get into a club. I leapt to my feet and ran to the front. The next half-hour was a bit of a blur, and I opened my eyes to find that I was laid out on the ground with my mates standing over me. I had met with the Lord in a powerful way and knew my lifestyle had to change.

Later that week I met two people who would have a huge influence on the future direction of my life, and would start me off on my mission to club culture. The first was Cameron Dante, a Radio 1 DJ and member of Christian dance act the World Wide Message Tribe. I chatted with him about my life, about how I'd fit back into conventional church, and how I needed help if I was to see my clubbing mates' lives changed as well. He pointed me towards Andy Hunter, another DJ who could relate to my teenage years. Andy told me about NGM, an arts and media charity based just outside Bristol. We exchanged numbers and went our separate ways, but a week later I received a phone call inviting me to an audition at NGM. I went to Bristol that Friday, got accepted, and moved to start at NGM on Sunday. It was a crazy whirlwind of a few days, but I knew it was time to change.

The Rubiks Cube

Years passed and I was a reformed human being. The teaching, mentoring and discipleship I received at NGM was amazing. I had also trained as a studio engineer, and had finally mastered the art of DJing. Once again a passion rose up in my heart for clubbers, for those people who felt like I had, years before, that life started and finished at the weekend, who couldn't wait for their next trip, who were lost in a world of binge drinking, sex, drugs, and drum & bass. It was clear to me God had put these people on my heart not just to pray and intercede for them, but to do something to help change their lives.

This is where the vision for The Rubiks Cube was born. I gathered together with others who had a similar heart and who enjoyed dance music. We started to pray, fast and seek ways in which we could impact clubland. As a DJ, I started to play for a number of different clubs and promoters in the city, and built some key relationships. On the back of this we decided to set up our own club night. Wanting to make sure we got the right venue, we spent weeks prayer-walking around the city and eventually narrowed the list down to three possible venues. Unfortunately, the one we had our hearts set on was only available on Mondays – but after further prayer, we decided to make this the home for The Rubiks Cube. The vision wasn't to run an overtly Christian night, but to maintain the quality of an underground night, run by a bunch of Christians. So we had people praying, others building relationships, some DJing, and some making themselves available to chat – but most of all, everyone was stepping out of their comfort zones to be Jesus-like to as many people as possible within club culture.

We named our night The Rubiks Cube after looking through an old box of toys and junk from my childhood. I found a tatty old Rubik's Cube, and it occurred to me what we wanted from the night was to impact different people from different backgrounds, who would come together in unity just like the cube – when all the colours are brought together, the unit is complete. Pretty cheesy I know, but at least it's not just a throwaway name – at least we can reference it to something.

Ups and downs

It was amazing how quickly word spread about this little drum &
bass night on Mondays. We had a great vibe, were getting some
major headline acts to play, and soon the club was packed week in
week out, bringing us huge financial gain. We decided very early on
our profits would be used to bless Bristol-based charities and organizations – those working with prostitutes, kids who had been kicked
out of school, the homeless, and many others. This made the whole
adventure even more rewarding.

Following the success of the night, and some good press in various
drum & bass magazines, local newspapers and websites, The Rubiks
Cube rapidly became one of the major players on the Bristol scene.
Using this reputation, I decided to try to get all the promoters in town
to work more closely together. I invited them all round one night and,
with everyone sitting in my front room with my special homemade
curry on their laps, we talked, laughed and came to an arrangement
that we would respect each other's nights, improve communication so
our events wouldn't clash, and put each other on our guest-lists. It was
amazing how a curry night saw the birth of a community. People
knew what we were about, and we regularly had people phone us
with prayer requests: we had recovering drug addicts asking for help;
we saw the lost and hurting wanting to find out what this special
something we had was, desperately wanting it for themselves.

We started up DJ cell-groups, where we would talk about God
and what he wants to do in our lives, discuss lifestyle issues,
and basically take people on a journey of discovery of what it is to
know Christ. It was an amazing time, and we saw many come
through. At one point we also had a prayer hotline, where we gave
our mobile numbers out with the offer of 24/7 prayer – we were
astounded by how many calls we got, with problems ranging from
family issues to broken relationships. It was an amazing tool with
lasting effects, and we even set up an internet message board where
people could post prayers, or ask for help and advice.

One particular prayer-request we received was from a local promoter. He had promoted a failed night at a club in Bristol that was

owned by the Greek mafia, and had lost them almost £5,000 in the process. They offered him two options – the first was the hospital, and the second was to sell drugs to pay off his debts. Not wanting to end up smashed to pieces, he was forced to work on the streets, and this was when we got the call asking for prayer. We offered him the best advice we could, and told him we would be there for him 24/7, praying our hearts out. Soon things took a turn for the better, the club laid off our mate, and his boss was arrested for drug trafficking and violent behaviour. It was wonderful to have our prayers answered, and to see the trust grow between him and us.

We experienced some huge ups and huge downs while running The Rubiks Cube. It was both a hilarious and tough journey, and we really had our eyes opened. It wasn't always easy; sometimes we were confronted with drunks, sometimes we got embroiled in scuffles with guys beating up their girlfriends. We saw punch-ups, people being bottled, and windows being smashed. It didn't help matters that we didn't find out until much later that one of Bristol's biggest underground drug operations was taking place in the club! We definitely faced our fair share of opposition.

Some of our nights didn't go to plan. On a number of occasions we had fewer than 20 people through the doors, having paid a big-name DJ hundreds of pounds to play. On these nights we were left considerably out of pocket, especially as sometimes we even had to refund people's entrance money for it being such a washout. I remember one particular night when our main DJ was kicked out by the bouncers after they caught him sniffing cocaine off a grubby toilet seat. This wasn't the first time this had happened, but this occasion left me totally in the deep end, faced with 200 paying clubbers with no guest DJ to play for them. Fortunately, I knew a few local celebrity DJs by this time, so I put in the call and managed to get one of them to cover. After coming so close to being a complete nightmare, the night ended up being a huge success.

Other times things didn't work out so well, such as the night when a sewer broke and the toxic smell filled the club, which was at full capacity for a Brazilian DJ playing in Bristol for the first time. The club cleared, the story spread, and for weeks afterwards we had incredible difficulty getting people to come back.

Perfect timing

One of the biggest challenges in the history of The Rubiks Cube came from within, in the form of one of the club's bouncers – a five-and-a-half foot, 22-stone, no necked, skinhead, hard-ass Scotsman called Ray. His past included multiple family problems, gang-related violence, regular run-ins with the police, a spell in the army, and dealing with the memory of people he had killed. Our main goal at The Rubiks Cube was to build relationships with the people we came into contact with, and Ray was to be no exception. This wasn't easy to begin with, since the most we ever heard come out of his mouth was a few words of filth; he would never look us in the eye, and at times he was threatening towards the team. After about six months, though, Ray started to show signs of change – we managed to have conversations that lasted more than a single sentence, had the occasional glimpse of eye-contact, and he started asking questions about why we were doing what we did. Over the following months our friendship grew, and then he dropped a bombshell. Before the club filled up one night, he told us that he needed prayer (we had offered to pray with him almost every week) because he had just been diagnosed with skin cancer, and the doctors had given him less than three months to live. Shortly after this he was admitted to hospital, and was soon bedridden. For such a proud, so-called hard man, this was torture – and we really felt his pain. During one of our prayer sessions we felt God call us to focus our energies on prayer and support for Ray. We decided to visit him daily, bringing gifts of ice-lollies, DVDs, and even a Bible.

I remember one muggy summer's day, when I went to the hospital for my visit. It was a Friday afternoon and we were in the middle of watching a film, when Ray turned to me and said, 'You know what you guys have, I want it!' I was gobsmacked. We spent a while talking about Jesus, and then we prayed together. Close to tears myself, I saw Ray's sincerity as he prayed for salvation with a tear rolling down his cheek. Later, as I was leaving, Ray turned to me with a smile and asked whether I'd be in the next day. I had family commitments that particular weekend, so told him I'd see him next week. The following Monday I called to let him know that I was on my way, but his mobile was answered by the ward nurse, who told me Ray had passed away during the night. I was devastated. But to this day I have the lasting memory of him pouring out his heart to God, and I know that everything was in God's perfect timing.

Ibiza

By now we had a vision that was pretty firmed up, and there was huge interest in it from all over. People with similar hearts for seeing God impact club culture wanted to take The Rubiks Cube model and run with it in their own cities. We never claimed it would work in other places, simply that we had seen some success in Bristol – but soon The Rubiks Cube was born in Birmingham, Swansea and, during the summer months, Ibiza.

In 2002, 24-7 Prayer took a team of Christian clubbers out to Ibiza to work alongside the church in trying to make an impact on the island's club scene (see Chapter 15). Ibiza is the clubbing capital of the world, with hundreds of thousands of clubbers descending on the island every summer, so you can imagine the hedonistic lifestyle of drink, drugs, sex and debauchery. We took a team out and managed to get a break at Mambo, one of the most prestigious clubs in the world, and there we ran The Rubiks Cube for many weeks. We played good soulful house music, with live percussionists and vocalists, while thousands of clubbers gathered along the beach to watch the sun set – it was the ideal setting. With a team praying onsite, and others prayer-walking and making themselves available to anyone who needed prayer or assistance, the vision was in full effect. We built long-lasting relationships with clubbers, managers, bar-staff, bouncers and promoters. One particular memory I have of our time in Ibiza was of a guy who had moved to the island to get away from his heroin addiction in London. His life was in shreds, and he had left his fiancée and kid behind. We got to know him well, and took it upon ourselves to work with him, love him, and let him know about the freedom that lies in Christ. One evening we had the most amazing conversation – something had stirred in his heart during the time we had known him, and he was desperate to find out about God. He could scarcely believe he could still be loved after everything he had done. Later that same night he was hit by a truck and killed. This was so hard to take in, but I have never forgotten his desperation to know more about the love of God, and my prayer is that the cover of God's grace would have taken this broken soul to be with him.

Where are we now?

Aside from a few blips, I am convinced the struggle of planting church into that club was worth all the sweat and tears. When I say 'planting church', I don't mean physically building a building – I mean planting the *heart* of the church, which is the people. Just as Jesus went to the people, so we took the church to them. Although I still think there is a place for a church in a building, I am convinced we must meet the needs of those outside the walls of those buildings. So many people, especially young people and clubbers in their late-teens and twenties, find church less and less relevant to their lives – so why insist that they must come to something they won't enjoy, when we can bring the essence of church (the good news, community, worship, relationships) to clubs?

Years down the line, our Rubiks Cube vision remains, although there is much work still to be done. If I could do it all again, I might have done some things differently – most importantly, I wouldn't have taken it all so seriously. I would have tried to enjoy the whole adventure a bit more. Heading up various nights across the country, I let myself get incredibly stressed instead of giving the teams more space to realize their own potential. I've made mistakes, but we've stuck at it – and we've seen some amazing things happen. It makes me sad when I see people come up with projects/ideas/ways to plant church, but then get bored and pack it in. I feel this is what God has called me to for life. I don't really care whether what I do is cutting edge or pioneering; all I care about is people, and for now the club nights remain the right vessel for me to build relationships across my city.

Mission doesn't have just one way of working. Over time, I've had all sorts of ideas: some of them have fallen flat on their faces, while others have made a major difference in people's lives. The key is that we go to the needs of the mission field, which could just as well be on our doorsteps as on the other side of the world. It's about showing love, compassion and kindness, as well as seeing people come to know Jesus as their saviour.

6

Nightshift

JON OLIVER (BOURNEMOUTH)

We found David slumped in a doorway outside the club at two o'clock in the morning, covered in his own vomit and unable to stand. He was a big chap, taller than my 6 feet, and twice as wide across the shoulders. I hesitated before approaching him, because occasionally people get stroppy about us sticking our noses in, and I didn't fancy the idea of this man-mountain kicking off. But this is what we're here for, I reminded myself, and gently shook him round. We sat him up and gave him a bottle of water to wash out his mouth, told him who we were, and asked if there was anything we could do to help – walk him home, phone a friend, whatever. However, the only thing he seemed interested in was the fact I was a chaplain. His ears pricked up, he shook his head clear, and told us he wanted to go to church.

I told him if he wanted to pray, he didn't have to go to anywhere special, that we could pray with him there and then. After all, I explained, church is not just a building, but is wherever two or three of us are gathered together in the name of Jesus. But David didn't give a monkey's about that. He just wanted to go to church.

He was adamant, so with one arm slung over my shoulder to steady himself, and with his vomit splattered all over us both, we negotiated our way through the crowds, past the clubs, and along to the local church. As soon as we were inside, David dragged himself to the front, knelt down on the floor, and began to weep. We sat nearby and prayed for him as he cried his eyes out; mumbling, praying, asking God for forgiveness. After a while, he picked himself up and we sat together in the pews, where we prayed and chatted for another hour or so. David told us a lot about himself in that time, about his young family, his issues with parenthood, and his understanding of God – and we were able to offer some insights into his situation, and a few words from God. By the end of our conversation, David had sobered up enough to get himself back to his hotel safely, so we walked him to the taxi rank and said goodbye, offering him some final words of encouragement. The following week he tracked us down to say thank you – in fact, we stayed in touch for a long time, sharing with one another the highs and lows of life, parenting, church, and walking with God.

Nightclub chaplaincy

This is a snapshot of what we do in Bournemouth. We wander around town every weekend (sometimes in the clubs, sometimes just outside them, sometimes in dark alleyways and side streets, sometimes in a church in the middle of the night) offering a helping hand and a listening ear, looking out for people in trouble, and coming alongside them in their spiritual journeys. Despite its relatively small size and its traditional associations with the blue-rinse brigade, Bournemouth has one of the biggest clubbing scenes in the UK. There are nearly 100 pubs, clubs and late-night bars in the town centre, with over 50,000 people out every week – many of them craving something more than the daily grind, hoping for some sort of meaningful experience.

Although an ever-increasing number of people seem to be open to spirituality, very few will seriously consider turning to the church for guidance or companionship in their spiritual journeys, and fewer still will ever bother turning up to a Sunday morning service. However, when I meet people like David, I am reminded and encouraged that the church has not lost its place in the social and spiritual consciousness of our society quite yet – in fact, often it is still the primary reference point for people when they think about religious or spiritual matters. For me, this is what being a club chaplain is all about. If people won't come to us, we'll go to them.

Background

I'm getting ahead of myself here, so let's back up a little. A few years ago, the rector of a church in the heart of Bournemouth town centre recognized the need to develop an appropriate response to the growing problems within the town's nightlife. A committee was formed and, working together with a number of local churches, they raised enough funding to employ the country's first nightclub chaplain. Three years later I took over the position.

When I look back, it sometimes seems as if all I did for the first few months was have loads of nights out on the expense account, running around telling everyone that I was getting paid to go clubbing! When I dig a little deeper, though, I remember I was actually spending this time sussing out the lie of the land, getting to know the people and the culture, and gathering together with like-minded Christians to build teams willing to invest themselves in this mission (many of whom had been involved long before I turned up). Together we were laying the groundwork for the next stage, and for months on end we prayed in and around the clubs and bars, lifting up God's name in places where usually all manner of other things are worshipped in his place.

Soon we decided to start working with more sense of purpose, and began developing a number of teams to go out clubbing every week. I contacted the managers of the three biggest clubs in town, and was amazed by their willingness to welcome us in. The manager of the most popular club not only gave us free entry, but also offered us complimentary drinks, and let us have the use of a room just off the main dancefloor in case someone needed to talk to us in private. In a short while we had three different teams going along to some of the messiest nights in town, plus a small group of us had set up our own club night in the basement of a bar in the town centre.

Rethinking the plan

After a few months, our club night proved financially unviable, so we took the difficult decision to shut it down. Some time later I started having misgivings about our clubbing teams too. What had begun as a dynamic, incarnational attempt to engage with clubbers on their own turf had gradually become more like cold-contact evangelism, with our teams prowling the clubs looking for people to pounce on. Although we had many great conversations and opportunities to pray with and for people in the clubs, I began to feel that if all we were offering were words, then these would become just one more opinion, one more voice, to get lost among countless other voices. St Francis' exhortation to 'preach the gospel at all times, if necessary use words' may have become somewhat of a cliché these days, but I am sure that – like so many clichés – this is probably because it contains a lasting truth which can impact every succeeding generation. It seems to me that if we come simply to preach, our words will be empty, but if we come to serve and love, our words will become imbued with a power beyond words.

As we began to think about where and how we could serve, it occurred to me that most people manage to hold it together while they're inside the clubs, but that it's when they leave and are wandering around the streets, or trying to get home, that many need a helping hand or listening ear. Around this time I heard about the Street Pastors, who were developing a pioneering ministry on the streets of inner-city London. Their work among young people and gang culture has had a phenomenal effect on the nightlife of the capital (and beyond), and so, after visiting their head office to pick up some tips, we decided to take our work out on the streets.*

It didn't take long to make the transition out on to the streets. We gathered together a team, mostly made up of people already involved with the work, and got a few jackets printed with 'Club

---

* I'd like to quickly clarify here that I don't object to the principle of working inside clubs. It was simply that at this time, and in this place, we felt we'd grown stale.

chaplain' emblazoned across the back (the pockets of which we filled with first-aid kits, tissues and bottles of water). Next we contacted the relevant agencies to let them know we'd be out and about at the weekends. The hardest part was saying goodbye to Slinky, my favourite club night, the first we'd worked at in an official capacity, and which we'd been going to every Friday for nearly two years. But it was worth it, because literally overnight our opportunities to love and serve people in need doubled, tripled, even quadrupled!

So what does the work actually look like?

A typical night with the club chaplain team starts at about 10pm with a cuppa and a pray, before we put on our uniforms and head into town. Often our evenings start slowly, as the real trouble generally kicks off in the small hours of the morning, so usually we wander about town for a while chatting to a few of the bouncers, regulars, managers and promoters we know. We have a vague route we usually stick to, taking us past almost every bar and club in the town centre – plus various parks, alleyways and side-roads that people sometimes manage to stagger down before slumping into a heap. It can take from an hour to the whole night to walk around town, depending on how many people we come across, and as the night progresses we usually find more people in all sorts of situations where we can help out.

Sometimes we find people collapsed in alleyways, with no idea how they got there, or sobbing in doorways, lost and alone. Other times we meet people who want to stay up all night, chatting about the meaning of life and setting the world to rights. Sometimes we pick people up out of the gutter, sometimes we give people a shoulder to cry on, and sometimes we end up giving people a lift home because they're in a vulnerable situation. Often it's people who have simply had too much to drink and are in no fit state to get home safely – and we can help out by simply walking them to meet their friends or to a taxi rank. We don't usually give people a lift home (not wanting to become known as some sort of free taxi service), but we do make an exception if there seems to be no alternative. One night we came across a couple who were pretty upset – the woman was pregnant and had just been beaten up. Her ankles were swollen and she was exhausted, but they didn't have any money, so we hopped in my car and drove them home. The father-to-be took one of my cards and we arranged to meet up the following week.

Our work isn't just about getting people home safely though; at times we are able to reach into people's lives and offer far more. One night we were walking past a multi-storey car-park when we heard the sound of sobbing from far above us. We hurried into the building, and climbed several floors before we found the source of the wails – a girl collapsed on the floor. When she saw us she scrambled to her feet, and my female team-mate threw her arms around her, then simply held her until the sobs subsided. It turned out that the girl, Stephanie, had been in an abusive relationship which had ended badly that night. As we talked to her, it became clear she assumed she needed the affirmation (however distorted and abusive) of a boyfriend in order to feel good about herself. She didn't seem to realize she had any other options – that she didn't have to sell herself short in this way. If we are called to make the teachings about our Saviour attractive (Titus 2.10), then this can't just be about fancy lighting or new technology in our church services – it has to be about presenting the good news in a light that truly reflects the fact that it *is* good news. To most of those we meet, the idea of pre-marital celibacy is not particularly attractive, and is not our number one selling point. However, to others, such as Stephanie, the possibility simply hasn't occurred to them – and the opportunity, the 'permission' almost not to have to give themselves up so easily, can be deeply attractive.

As Christ first loved us

Another time, we came across a lad called Mark who was bleeding profusely and throwing up behind one of the clubs. As we helped him pick himself up, he tried to piece together what had happened, and realized he'd had his drink spiked by a girl who'd been trying to chat him up. Eventually one of his friends turned up and, as he and I stood chatting, we watched my team-mate show Mark how to stop his nose bleeding, while she continued to clean him up. As she knelt down in front of him, washing his face, his shirt, his hands, and even his feet, Mark's friend and I suddenly stopped talking, absorbed by the scene of my team-mate washing Mark's feet, serving him in such a Christ-like way. Immediately our conversation turned from idle banter to deeper subjects – about what we were doing and why. He kept asking, 'Why?' Why were we doing this? Why were we out in the middle of the night? Why were we willing to put ourselves out to help a stranger? I was able to share with him that we are called to love others as Christ first loved us, and that we were doing our best to do just that – but that whatever we do, nothing can ever match the love of God that is revealed in Jesus. We talked for a while longer and then saw them safely home.

Of course, it hasn't all been so positive. There are regularly long, boring nights when nothing seems to happen. Then there are the nights when we get people shouting at us or acting aggressively (usually because they have a problem with Christianity or religion in general, rather than with us personally). There are also nights when I've been assaulted – I've been punched in the face a few times, had my nose broken, and on one occasion someone tried to bottle me and threatened me with a knife. One of my best friends always tells me that in these situations I should count myself lucky, reminding me that the disciples rejoiced that they were counted worthy of suffering for the sake of Jesus (Acts 5.40ff). I can see his point, but have to admit I don't always remember to count myself lucky when nursing a black eye or a broken nose!

Becoming established within the nightlife

On the whole, though, we have seen real success since we took the work out on the streets. So much so, that we've gradually gained recognition from others working in the nightlife – a large number of managers have agreed to have our posters and contact details displayed inside their clubs, and some have invited us in to offer our services to their staff. The ambulance service has expressed an interest in seeing how we can work closer together; and the police are trying to secure us additional funds, having recognized the part we play in indirectly reducing crime levels. Even the council seems to be fully behind our work – offering both support and funding, and inviting us to join them in developing new projects. We've also had several news crews follow us around for a weekend or two, trying to capture on film what all the buzz is about.

We've also been blessed with ever-increasing support from local churches. What started off as a handful of congregations supporting the work has become over 20 churches from across town and across the denomination spectrum. Likewise, what began as a handful of friends has become a team of nearly two dozen volunteers from all over Bournemouth and beyond.

He sent them out two by two

One of the things I tell new volunteers is that they should feel able to be fully themselves when working with the club chaplain team – that there is no set way of doing things, no special words to say or formula for success. We usually work in pairs (sometimes just two of us out, sometimes more) and I am always partnered with new volunteers for their first few sessions on duty, meaning I'm there to back them up as they explore how to approach the work for themselves. Since we're all different, with varying gifts, ideas, experiences and passions to bring to the mix, I want everyone on the team to have the freedom to express their faith, and their willingness to serve others, in their own way.

Some team-members take a while to get to grips with it all, but others are willing to jump in feet first. One volunteer, on her first night out, was asked by a group of lads what we were doing – and before I could give my usual spiel, she told them that we were simply there to pray for people. Chris, the leader of the bunch, laughed out loud and said he was 'OK, thanks', but pushed his friend towards her, jokingly suggesting that he could do with some prayer. This lad looked as if he was about to run a mile. Fortunately he didn't; and, in spite of the initial laughter, we soon got into a real conversation with these lads. An hour later, two of them were praying with my team-mate, calling on God to reveal himself in their lives, with Chris shouting towards the heavens that he needed God. Meanwhile, the lad who'd nearly bolted at the beginning told me he'd never given a moment's thought to the possibility of God being real, but that our conversation had got him thinking that maybe there *could* be something beyond simply that which we can see or touch. A small step perhaps, but a first step none the less. The funny thing was we had started talking to these lads when they'd asked for directions to the nearest strip club, and by the time we said goodbye, after nearly three hours of prayer and conversation, it occurred to me that all the strip clubs would now be closed!

Transient culture

We never actually saw these lads again, and this is one of the things that I have found most difficult about working in the nightlife – it's often difficult to build continuity with people we meet. We always offer ongoing care and support, but Bournemouth has an enormous nightlife, and club culture can be so transient, with people travelling from all over the country for a night out, that often we don't meet the same people again. This can become pretty disillusioning after a while. On the other hand, there are others who we regularly see out and about. One of these is Susie, who we met when she was lost and alone one night, and helped find her friends. We hung around with them for a couple of hours, chatting about life, God, the universe and everything. For months afterwards we'd bump into Susie at weekends, or get a call from her in the middle of the night wanting to meet up – sometimes when she was depressed or in some sort of trouble, but often just to say hello.

Sometimes when we meet people more than once, it's clear the opportunity is there for a reason. One night we were walking through the town centre when we came across a couple of lads arguing. As we walked by, we saw that one was threatening the other with a bottle. Understandably, the police have asked us not to get involved in violent situations because, being untrained for this, we're just as likely to inflame the situation as to diffuse it. But suddenly I realized that we'd met this lad – Ethan – earlier that month so, calling out his name, we wandered over. Immediately his whole demeanour changed, and he quickly lost both the bottle and any interest in attacking the other lad. When we met Ethan the first time we'd spent a long time sharing our experiences and struggles with life and faith, and seemingly as a result of this he now felt able to trust us enough to open up about how he was feeling that night. Within a couple of minutes we were sitting down together as he tearfully told us how he'd lost his job and hadn't got a clue what the future held. After talking it through, he'd sobered up and calmed down enough to walk home without any trouble, so we said goodbye. Once again, it occurred to me that so many of the troubles we see at night (the arguments, the violence, the vandalism) are simply a result of the fact that so often people don't know how to deal with their problems in any other way.

Despite the police advice on staying out of violent situations, sometimes it's difficult *not* to intervene. We've come to be very wary of getting involved when a couple are having an argument, though, because they can be on the verge of tearing one another's throats out one minute, only to join forces and turn on us for sticking our noses in the next. But, to be honest, I'd rather risk humiliation or abuse than walk by when someone is in trouble. That said, I haven't always judged these situations as well as I did with Ethan. I remember one night when a complete stranger started behaving aggressively towards a man I was talking to – but clocking my uniform, he clearly decided I was the easier target, and all of a sudden he swung for me with a bottle. By the grace of God, or by virtue of being sober, my reflexes were quicker than his and I was able to dodge his attack. Unfortunately, when his bright-blue drink spilled out of the bottle and all over his clean white shirt, I was unable to stifle a small laugh. This enraged him still further, and he decided he was going to stab me instead. However, as he went for his knife, one of the local homeless lads spotted what was going on and, bellowing something about not messing with 'his' chaplain, leapt towards my attacker and chased him off up the road.

Building relationships

Over time, we have seen a gradual shift in focus – from simply club-bers, to the whole range of people found within club culture and the nightlife: students, promoters, bouncers, bar-staff, managers, take-away staff, and the homeless. Sometimes a whole night now passes with us barely speaking to any clubbers, but instead wandering from club to bar to club to take-away shop, talking to the staff and regulars we know. A few of the bouncers seem to look forward to our visits, making sure we call in every time we're out. When I had a weekend off a few months after we'd started working the streets, I got an unexpected phone call from one of the bouncers at 2am – just wanting to check I was OK, as he hadn't seen me that night!

Unlike the clubbers who we often meet only once, we get to see the bouncers, managers and other staff week in week out, and have been able to build real, long-term relationships with some of them. Several have become firm friends, and we regularly meet up during the week for a drink or a bite to eat. Sometimes I'm even invited on staff nights out – during which I'm often poked, prodded and grilled as they try to work out if I'm 'for real'. They especially enjoy push-ing the boundaries of good taste to see if they can break me down – many of them being unable to reconcile themselves to the idea of a Christian out on the town having a good time. Some even seem surprised that I'm allowed to drink! One of my favourite bouncers also works at a gym during the day, and most weeks I head over there for a game of badminton.

Often one of the managers will pop over to my house for a cup of tea when we both finish work at 4am, to wind down before heading home. Sometimes we'll just share funny stories about the situations we've had to deal with that night, but other times we'll watch the dawn rise as we discuss the meaning of life and the possibility of God. Sometimes this means I don't get to bed until the rest of the country is getting up!

Another aspect of taking the work out on the streets is that we've got to know quite a few of the homeless people who hustle up a living in the nightlife. We have become friends with some of them;

others we have been able to serve practically (buying them something hot to eat, helping them fill in their benefit forms, or giving them lifts to hospital appointments); and some simply appreciate the opportunity to have a normal conversation, having been hassled by drunks all night. However, there are also those who relish the chance to discuss God, share stories of faith, and pray together. Alan's story in particular always sticks with me.

Alan and the organ

One night we were sitting on the front steps of a big church in the middle of town, chatting with Alan, one of the homeless lads we knew quite well. Alan had been on the streets for years and was an alcoholic, a heroin addict, and an agnostic – but during the year we'd known him, he'd become increasingly keen to get clean and more open to contemplating faith. After a few months he began asking us to pray with him quite regularly, and eventually admitted he had a vague belief in God but needed to experience him for himself before he could truly believe. That night, on the church steps, he seemed particularly desperate to turn his life around and have a fresh start.

Our conversation was suddenly interrupted by two things – the sound of the organ unexpectedly playing inside the church, and, moments later, the appearance of a young clubber pushing past us and trying to open the church door. When the clubber, Simon, realized it was locked he sat down dejectedly, so I asked him to tell us his story. He explained that sometimes he sat in the graveyard at night, to pray in peace and quiet. Simon usually didn't want to 'bother' God by sitting inside, he said, content to be within sight of the building, but that week he'd been having a tough time and had wanted to be closer to God. So, as he'd sat in the darkness outside the church, he'd quietly asked God if he could go inside – and at that exact moment, the organ had begun to play.

Simon took this to be an answer to prayer, permission from God to go inside, and as I watched the excitement battle with disappointment on his face, who was I to disagree? I took the church key out of my pocket, opened the door, and invited them in. It turned out the organist had been unable to sleep, and had decided to come to the church at 2am to practise! He continued to play as we found somewhere to sit. My team-mate sat with Simon, and for over an hour explained the gospel, talked through his questions about God, then prayed with him. Meanwhile, I continued to chat to Alan.

I was struck by how closely Alan's words about a fresh start echoed Jesus' promise of a new life, so I explained that everything he said he wanted – to start afresh, to be cleaned and healed from within – was exactly what Jesus came to offer. Alan asked if we could pray, and as we did I begged Jesus to reveal himself, to touch Alan's life. After a while we fell silent and I waited to see what would happen. Eventually Alan lifted his head and, with eyes and smile wide, he leaned over and whispered, 'This is f***ing better than heroin, Jon.' Before I had a chance to reply, he continued, 'And I'm not tripping or anything, mate, but it's like there's a whole load of people stood around, telling me I'm on the right path now.' I tried to explain that this was Jesus making himself known, but Alan cut me off, bluntly informing me he already knew that. He was so excited he wanted to go outside and pour his booze down the drain right away, and was desperate to find a Bible and get stuck into it immediately.

We left the church in a glow, and the following day I met Alan and bought him a Bible. The week after that he checked into rehab. A year down the line, Alan still battles the bottle sometimes, but he's off the streets, clean from heroin, reunited with his young family, and has a real faith in God. Sometimes this business we're in is a gradual process, often depressingly slow, and we have to be willing to be in it for the long haul if we hope to see lasting change in people's lives. As for Simon, we never heard from him again, although I still remember to pray for him from time to time.

Where do we go from here?

To be honest, I'm not sure. I haven't got some grand plan. I haven't got the next five years mapped out. I haven't got a bunch of objectives and criteria to be ticked off on a checklist. After all, when I look back over the last five years, I can see that very little has panned out in the way I thought it would. We do have some ideas in the pipeline – continuing to explore how church might look within club culture, developing an increased internet presence, starting up new club teams, maybe running another club night – but who knows how any of this will work out?

One thing I am sure of is that it gets to the point when we need more than just words – the words we say are important, but they need to be backed up with actions. However, words and actions are not enough in themselves (there are lots of people saying good things and doing good things), and it gets to the point when we realize that nothing *we* can do compares to seeing the power of God reach into people's lives. God chooses to use us in his mission, but we must never forget this is his mission – we are simply invited along for the ride. Our task is to keep our eyes and our hearts open to the prompting of the Spirit, to try our best to see where God is at work, and to join him in his mission to this culture, to these people, to this lost generation.

7

The Malt Cross

DAVE WARD (NOTTINGHAM)

I remember the night very clearly. The café-bar had not been open in the evenings for very long, and I decided to introduce myself to the DJ for the night. But as soon as I said hello, he turned to me and said, 'Look, I know that this place is run by Christians, and I just want you to know that I am not at all interested in God, so please don't start.' I told him that was fine, that I really had come over simply to introduce myself, and that if he didn't want to talk about God it was OK by me.

For me this little story sums up what we do at the Malt Cross, a café-bar in the heart of the city centre in Nottingham. This place is an amazing Grade II listed building, an old-time music hall built in 1877 and reopened in 2003 by a consortium of local churches and the Church Army. Our aim is to be a sanctuary, a place of rest and safety, as well as a beacon of hope and a positive influence on the people in and around it.

If you were to enter the building and take a couple of minutes to admire the décor and architecture (in particular the large glass dome roof), you might think that it was just another trendy city centre café-bar. We're open from 11am until 11pm, and alongside our great menu of healthy food and amazing coffees we serve alcohol. Yes that's right, a sanctuary, a safe place, a Christian-run project – and *alcohol*. From the beginning, the café-bar team wanted the Malt Cross to be a bar run by Christians rather than a Christian bar. It needed to be well run and have a distinctiveness that set it apart from other bars, but we didn't want to exclude people, or feed people's prejudices of Christians by being something that would not relate to non-churchgoers. So there are no posters, no leaflets, and no clever tracts that give our little secret away!

'Secret?' I hear you cry, 'But surely the gospel isn't a secret?' Yes, that's true, but as with all the best-kept secrets, someone will eventually tell. In this case, the secret is being spread by people who aren't churchgoers, people like the DJ above who love to tell their mates that this is a bar run by Christians because, in his words, 'I love to see the shock on their faces when they find out! So please don't put leaflets out, or you'll spoil my fun.' So here we have the unchurched telling their mates what we are about. Wow! What an amazing advert for the church.

To carry on with the DJ's story: a couple of weeks after our initial 'conversation', he suddenly asked me whether I knew of any spiritual directors. I told him I didn't, but asked why he might be interested. 'Well, I think that my house might be haunted,' he said, 'and I'm having real problems sleeping at night.'

'Have you tried praying about it?' I asked.

'Yeah, I have, but it just seems to get worse when I do.'

'Would you like a couple of us to pray for you?'

'What would that entail, me sitting in the corner of a room while you guys pray for me?'

'Well, something like that,' I said, realizing that the whole concept of prayer is very different when you are from outside the church environment. He agreed to give it a go, and I suggested he came down the following evening so we could spend some time together. That night I prayed for him my whole way home, although I have to admit that I was pretty surprised when he turned up the following evening. *I* hadn't forgotten, but I had expected *him* to have! I asked him how his night had been. 'It was amazing,' he replied, 'the house was really peaceful and I had the best night's sleep ever!' When I saw him the next week his very first comment was, 'That prayer stuff really works, this whole week has been amazing!' Since then we have regular chats about God, he has become far more open about faith, and his journey has begun to move in a new direction.

The background

Upwards of 70,000 people are out in Nottingham city centre each week on Friday and Saturday nights, and a great many of these people are susceptible to drug and alcohol abuse. Before the 1990s, shoppers and workers went home at around 5pm, and then there was a lull until a few people came back to go to the theatre or cinema, or maybe to use the restaurants and pubs. On the whole it was a pretty calm place in which to be in the evening. Over the last decade, the landscape has greatly changed, and Nottingham city centre now has a vibrant night-time economy which continues to grow at an alarming rate. Legislation has shifted, and greater operating freedom has meant that Nottingham now has a much wider range of clubs, pubs, cafés and restaurants on offer.

Across the UK, city and suburban residents are raising concerns that city centres have become 'no go areas' in the evenings. They are worried about the large numbers of people congregating, and the increasing threat of antisocial behaviour. However, an active night-time economy shouldn't necessarily amount to mayhem or compromise safety, but all too often cities don't have sufficient structures in place to manage the growth and give people the support they need. The concept of a 24-hour economy seems unlikely to go away as it is a consumer-driven market, and businesses will naturally respond to such demands. The challenge for the church and other support organizations is adapting how and when they work in order to meet people's ever-changing needs, presented by our ever-changing context.

The Malt Cross

Following its nineteenth-century beginnings as a music hall, the Malt Cross passed through numerous hands (among other things becoming a burlesque, and later a non-alcoholic bar) before being refurbished to its original state by the Malt Cross Music Hall Trust in the mid-90s. Despite their best efforts, it was forced to close in

1999 as a result of mounting financial losses, but the trustees worked hard to safeguard the building's future use so the Trust's original objectives could continue.

In 2002, a student at St John's Theological College in Nottingham, who had previously worked for the Trust, wrote a dissertation on Fresh Expressions of church, using the Malt Cross as a model. He took the finished work to the principal who agreed it needed to be made a reality rather than remaining a theory. Soon a number of church leaders and previous trustees were contacted, a management group was set up, and in November 2003 the Malt Cross reopened as a café-bar in the heart of the city centre. Five churches from four denominations, along with St John's College, the University Chaplaincy, and the Church Army, continue to support the work prayerfully, practically and financially.

The vision

In the midst of so many pubs, clubs and casinos, our vision is to work in partnership to change the atmosphere in Nottingham city centre – our hope is that the city will become a safer place for everyone through our influence on the lifestyle of the people connected with the Malt Cross. The aim is to 'be the best hosts we possibly can be by being a blessing to everyone we meet today'. This means valuing everyone who comes through the door, which can be anything up to 500 people each day, as the beloved human being they really are, rather than viewing them simply as customers, or even possible converts. It means being authentic and transparent, and acting with integrity in all aspects of our daily lives. It means being genuine in our friendships regardless of people's age, race, religious background or social status – what really matters is that, wherever possible, we invest in people and express the love of God. We are committed to seeking God, letting him influence and transform our lives, and crying out to him for our peers: 'Come, Holy God, let your presence fill this place, use us as you are at work here.'

This is not restricted to those who come through the doors of the Malt Cross, and soon after opening the café-bar we also started the community outreach work. The vision for this team is to be 'church on the streets' – making themselves available throughout the day, and especially on those busy nights when the city centre isn't necessarily at its best. The teams go out in pairs, to help those who have had too much to drink, to make sure people get home safely, to phone for ambulances, to help those who've been caught up in a fight, or to offer support and advice to people with drug and alcohol dependency problems, as well as those who find themselves living on the streets, or simply those who need a listening ear.

Through all of this, a number of us are developing a lifestyle of faith and looking at ways of developing Christ-centred missional communities in Nottingham. This doesn't mean there is any expectation that the people we come into contact with need to get 'all spiritual' – belonging is far from an 'all or nothing' proposition. Some people are neighbours, seen only in passing; some are regular partygoers who are just here for the vibe; some are committed to working together and contributing to the life of the Malt Cross; and other don't really care, and just want a coffee right now . . . and that's fine with us! Regardless of which category a person might fit into, they are welcomed as part of what we are doing. Our hope is that whatever happens it is comfortable yet meaningful – challenging and enabling us to grow into what God has intended us to be, to see what he is already doing in the lives of others, to join in with whatever he is doing, and to encourage it to grow and develop.

Sanctuary

We have always hoped the Malt Cross would be seen as a 'safe place' in the city, and are delighted when people comment on this – sometimes actually referring to it as a 'sanctuary'. Through this we have managed to meet the spiritual needs of many who have become disillusioned and are looking for something different from traditional organized religion, and have provided space for others to revive their faith in a supportive environment. We offer people freedom to express faith in an unconventional way, and not to feel as if they are being moulded by a system – allowing them to experiment with, and develop, their gifts in ways they hadn't been able to before. For these people, and others, we offer a refuge where they can 'be still' and discover – or rediscover – life with Christ, through being accepted, loved and welcomed. With its combination of café-bar hospitality and the prayer-room upstairs, many have likened it to a contemporary friary. It is a place of retreat, a base for training and mission, and a sanctuary in which to explore creative space, relational space, thinking space and sacred space.

Anne's story

'Without the Malt Cross, and the support and encouragement of its staff, I might never have found God and got through my depression.' In 2005 Anne became deeply depressed following the death of her grandfather (who was a real hero to her) and an accident that left her with limited mobility for many months. The previous year she had discovered the Malt Cross and, through becoming a regular, had built up a number of relationships with the team. These friends supported Anne through her depression by spending time with her, listening, praying and offering practical assistance. One day Anne decided she wanted to try some meditation, and visited the prayer-room at the Malt Cross. Here she met God in a powerful and intimate way, and felt him say, 'It is going to be OK. I know your struggles, you can ask me to help you.' From this moment Anne began to experience a joy and peace she had never known before. She began to explore and develop her new-found faith through the Malt Cross community, joined a church in the city, and is now actively involved in our community outreach work.

Small missional communities

The core of what we do, then, is rooted in relationship: our relationship with God, and our relationships with the people we come across, connect with, and invest in. This is always rooted in prayer, in allowing the Holy Spirit to do his thing, and in looking for opportunities to enable this. We have found that community is one of the best ways to enable this, and with Jesus planted firmly in the middle, this is powerful stuff. After all, God himself is a community of three, and as Jesus said, 'where two or three come together in my name, there am I with them' (Matthew 18.20). This is ultimate community; this is church.

As relationships continue to blossom, our vision is to see small missional communities emerge around the city, comprised of people who are committed to praying, being open with God and one another, to developing each other, and serving inside and outside these communities – in friendship groups, workplaces, communities and the whole city. The aim is to improve lives, give people purpose and direction, and ultimately bring people into a relationship with God through Christ. Our name for these missional communities is 'PODS', which is what we do when we get together for 'Prayer, Openness, Developing & Serving'.

PODS are intentionally missional, and focused on a place, project or people group. We have found that the fewer people there are in PODS, the easier it is to maintain cohesion, the more likely it is that people will take on responsibility, and the stronger they are in the areas of community, openness, confidentiality, flexibility, communication, direction and leadership. The structure is flexible enough to allow individuals to develop their own walk with God, allowing for freedom and spontaneity, while ensuring it is balanced with a healthy level of support and accountability. This is made easier through having shared aims and a statement that easily rolls off the tongue: 'Be still, be holy, and be available.' We feel this has the right balance of being unifying and biblical – it is about *being* church rather than *going* to church, allowing freedom through being low on control but high on accountability, and encouraging organic growth in each area of mission. This structure for growth takes a fivefold form:

1 We develop a personal pattern of prayer, openness and intimacy with God.
2 We spend time with a close friend with whom we can be totally open and honest.

3 We gather in small groups, PODS, for Prayer, Openness, Development & Service.
4 We participate in the shared life of the wider Malt Cross community.
5 We observe and gain experience in ministry and witness to 'pre-Christian' people.

Faye's story

In 1999, Faye's father was diagnosed with bowel cancer, and she was involved in nursing him right the way through to his premature death in 2004. She found this incredibly difficult, and that the only way she could make the pain go away was by spending the weekends in a haze of drugs and alcohol. Shortly before her dad died, a friend introduced Faye to the Malt Cross, and she soon became a regular visitor. Through her increasing involvement there, she widened her social network to include a whole bunch of people whose lives were not centred on drugs and alcohol. Their influence, friendship and encouragement helped her to get her alcohol consumption under control, become free of drugs, and get her life back on track. Faye has also rediscovered faith and become an active member of the Malt Cross community – she meets regularly with one of our PODS, and is training to join our community outreach team so she can help others who use drugs and alcohol in an attempt to drown their pain and difficulties.

Gatherings

We have tried to keep large group meetings to a minimum – we have a meal together once a month and share communion, but that is the only 'act of worship' we have as a whole group. We recognize the fact that particular forms of worship can be a delight for one person, but a drudgery for another. Ultimately our desire is for us all to live lifestyles of worship and to glorify God in and through our daily walk with him. Therefore our aim is to provide space for different forms of worship to develop out of the experiences and experimentations of each individual and group.

We have found that everyone enjoys eating together and that this, both for new and not-yet Christians, is a far less threatening environment to walk into than a room full of people following unfamiliar rituals and singing unfamiliar songs. I remember one particular meal together, where I invited everyone to take communion with whoever they were sitting beside. I had prepared slips of paper containing Jesus' words from the Last Supper, and simply let everyone get on with it in their own time. Earlier that evening, one young woman who was still discovering faith told me how she struggled with the seeming differences between the God revealed in the Old Testament and the God revealed in the New Testament – and I watched with excitement as she took communion with another young woman who was also in the process of discovering God. At the end of the meal, she came over and eagerly told me she had felt God answer her question in that moment of communion, and felt so much better for it. How easy was that! Why not let God do the hard work? Let's face it, he knows what he is doing. And who knows, we might be surprised at some of the radical new responses that come from people just setting out on their journey. As Vincent Donovan once wrote, 'Do not try to call them back to where they were, and do not try to call them to where you are, as beautiful as that place might seem to you. You must have the courage to go with them to a place that neither you nor they have ever been before.'[31]

What an adventure! What are we waiting for?

Come, Holy Spirit, do your stuff!

8
Shine Angel

GRAHAM ROBINSON (BELFAST)

It was a big night at Shine, the biggest club in Belfast. Held in the students' union of Queen's University, it has five rooms on three floors, loads of space, and endless stairs, corridors and sofas, where frazzled clubbers can crash to talk, recover and smile. The main room of Shine is a fantastic cavern of sound – underground, dark and brooding, with everyone consumed in their own worlds, dancing, dancing, dancing. It has always been a special place, with a genuine air of acceptance even in Belfast's darkest times. Maybe it was the Ecstasy, but I like to think it was a little bit of a cultural revolution going on in Belfast's clubland.

I was there with a bunch of friends, heroes of the dancefloor, and not the sort likely to show up in church. We chatted, hung out in the bar, scattered into the throngs of people to find different adventures, floors and DJs, then returned to find each other again. At about 1am, a few of us were dancing in our usual spot. I sometimes find it intimidating to worship God in front of non-Christians but, as the four or five friends around me were on something like 40 pills between them, it didn't seem such a problem.

So I opened myself up to the presence of God: head down, eyes closed, dancing hard, praying in tongues, feeling good. I suddenly had the sense I should look up at the ceiling. As I did, keeping my eyes shut, I became aware of an angel there. A huge ebony angel, powerful and strong, with his back flat against the ceiling and his arms spread out as if he was pulling the ceiling down. It seemed as if a huge trapdoor was being opened . . . *Where did it go? What was he opening?* The Heavens. I saw the glory of God inside, shining down into the club. It was bright, it was warm and it was wonderful. It spoke hope and blessing over everyone in the room. His presence and kingdom were invading the club.

Addicted to Bass

Some people love the mountains,
Some people are into golf,
Others prefer coffee and DVDs.

It's the drums that give me life,
A wall of sound puts a smile on my face.

Hundreds of people queue outside a club,
Their place of worship,
Electricity of expectancy,
Impatience and desire.

The bassline thumps,
The crowd jumps,
This my place
To be consumed by the presence of God.

In the midst of a dark dirty throbbing mass of people
I lose control in Worship,
Here I push my body to its limit in honour of our King.
Bring it on David and the heavenly angels,
For these few hours I challenge you
To a dance off.

Later on the house lights come on,
But everyone keeps on dancing,
Squeezing every last drop out of this encounter.
Mascara all down that girl's face,
Sweat in his hair,
A bright red face over there,
But no one cares.

We're all too busy grinnin'.

Well done Mr DJ,
A fine sermon of beats, rhythm and bass.

I step outside, the cold air bites,
Wrestling with burger vans,
Into a taxi,
Back home.

Sit back, relaxing into tomorrow,
Members of the congregation
Discuss how much it rocked our world.
What else is going on?

That's club culture to me. The same place where organized crime sells potentially fatal drugs to underage kids, where drinks are spiked, louts fight, and thugs are paid to control them. In this chapter I want to encourage Christian clubbers to keep going, and to explain why I do it. This encouragement is important, because it's hard being a Christian clubber. It's easy to doubt when you hear the lies that clubs aren't good places for Christians to be in, that they're too dangerous, that I should jack it all in, keep everyone happy, repress myself. But then I listen to 'Racing Green' by High Contrast, or the Thin White Duke remix of Royksopp's 'What Else is There?' and I just can't help but thank God that he made sequencers; can't help wonder what the Psalmists would have done with an 808 drum machine; can't fight the smile on my face when I see this vision of Jesus standing there nodding his head along to the beat going, 'OH YEAH!'

Who was Jesus? He was a man of such love that he was prepared to die for us because we need forgiveness. Who needs to hear that? Everyone. Where can we find millions of people who don't know that? In the nightlife. Did Jesus say go to all the world except clubs and tell them the good news of his love? No, of course not. He said, 'Go into the world. Go everywhere and announce the Message of God's good news to one and all' (Mark 16.15, MSG). So go on. Pick up your phone. Call directory enquiries. Ask them for the name of a local club. And then book a taxi . . .

I came to give you life

'I came to give you life to the full' – Jesus
'Christ in you the hope of Glory' – Paul
'Perfect love drives out fear' – John

Christ in me is the hope of Glory; a full life comes from knowing the passionate heart of God. The God who spoke this reality into existence, and burns with love for us. When we allow him to tell us he loves us and truly let it sink in, we can carry this in us and share it with others. And if you haven't experienced that yet, get into a place where you are alone and listen to Jesus.

Deep in the silence, his simple words:

'I love you.'
'No, I really love you.'
'No no, I really, really love you.'

This is the starting point, the beginning of life, love, and a true experience of Jesus. Don't be in a hurry to leave this place. Get addicted to it; let a desperate hunger grow from there. Allow yourself to be completely possessed by the Holy Spirit and God's love, so that you carry his presence, his acceptance, his love, with you wherever you go.

Once you have caught hold of who Jesus really is, it becomes very clear that, in comparison, the things *we* do really don't matter. Compared to the love of God and Jesus' victory on the cross, everything else is chasing the wind. Futile. So as soon as you feel as if you have to do something for God, return to that place of all-consuming love and realize you don't *have* to do anything. Instead, in his mercy, God *lets* us do things with him.

We are a living, breathing mess. Unpredictable, unproductive, selfish weirdos, trusted to usher in the sublime mysteries and raw supernatural power of heaven into the midst of our own little corners of planet Earth. You might not always feel like it, but that's his will. And it is beautiful! So we just need to listen out, and go on adventures. In his love and power, we get to destroy the works of the devil (1 John 3.8), and then a certain kind of fire begins to pump through our veins . . . suddenly the concept of dancing for eight hours to celebrate him doesn't seem so strange; and half an hour of soft rock each week doesn't seem quite enough to express the praise that's due Jesus Christ the Lord.

We have repressed so much in our Western church that we have severed key elements of our humanity. Dancing is good for you, losing control is essential. We must re-embrace the fullness of our humanity, the full life Jesus offers. This includes rediscovering elements of our creativity and our sexuality that we have been too afraid of making a mistake with to live fully. Christians often seem keen to point out that faith is not a list of rules – but what are we living in reality, what example do we give with our actions? If we continue to hold back in fear, how will we move on to live life as Jesus did? Secure enough in his sexuality to be able to hang out with prostitutes and not give in to temptation. Passionate enough to be enraged, to pick up a whip when he saw people misusing the temple.

Church

In club culture I have discovered forms of community where people are meeting each other's needs in a radically different environment. Aspects of Christ's character, which the church seems to have forgotten, are alive and well in the nightlife.

The best parts of club culture are totally inclusive – if you dance, if you connect with the music, you are welcome; you are one of us. You don't have to prove yourself or be a regular, just being there is enough to be welcomed. But it's more than just that – club culture can be very open, vulnerable and generous. Buying someone you have just met a drink is commonplace, sharing drugs that might have cost £100 is no problem. There is something in the act of two strangers meeting at a club for only a few hours, and then being prepared to give their whole body to the other person, that is so intimate, so fragile, so abandoned; they risk it all with each other. Obviously casual sex is very damaging and not part of God's plan, but there are elements of risk and abandonment alive in club culture that are quintessentially part of our humanity.

We must be reawakened to the intimacy of our sacraments. Shouldn't the sharing of communion, the body and blood of Christ, provoke a stronger unity than the sharing of drinks and drugs among clubbers?

Why do I love club culture? Maybe it's because I can meet people who are not so afraid of making a mistake that they never take a risk. The Holy Spirit in us is more euphoric than ten pills, more affirming than a pound of coke, more exhilarating than a yard of speed – but how many of us have searched deeply enough in the love of Christ to be that free and wild? Unless we have had the embrace of God take our breath away, how can we tell a guy on ketamine he's wasting his time? Sometimes I think that some Christians are so opposed to clubbing outreach because we encounter people there more alive than we are. It's a lot easier to write them off than ask Jesus why *we* aren't experiencing the life of fullness he came to give.

Communion on the dancefloor

I started clubbing when I was fifteen, before my voice had broken. There was a nightclub nicknamed The Crèche, which let anyone in. For the rest of my teenage years I went clubbing, chasing meaning and acceptance in girls, drinks and drugs. But slowly I began experiencing God's love in a powerful way – more powerfully than anything I had experienced on a night out.

Soon I began to get my satisfaction and affirmation from God rather than clubbing, for a while I went through a phase of holding off clubbing, and an overly religious sense of what seemed right and wrong took over. But I knew that Jesus wanted my friends to get to know him too, and that if I separated myself off into a Christian bubble I might never see them again. Particularly while I was at university, it seemed incredibly important to go to the union, the bars and the clubs to avoid isolation and irrelevance.

So I continued going clubbing, with more confidence in Jesus' strength than concern about my weaknesses. Heading out with Christian friends helped to keep the focus, and to pick up the pieces when things went wrong. Mission trips with 24-7 Prayer to Miami and Ibiza (see Chapter 15) helped me work out more what it means to be Jesus within club culture. Throughout this time there were highs and lows, many mistakes and failures, but we celebrated, we danced, we lived.

A few years ago, a church in Belfast had a small team of praying clubbers. Meeting once a month with a meal, sharing together and then heading out, their hope was to communicate Jesus' love to some of Belfast's clubbers. Some people went into the club, while others prayer-walked the surrounding area. This group sowed richly into the nightlife but eventually dispersed, although not before I got to know a few of those involved. One night I was heading out to Shine with my usual friends, and I felt like inviting along a couple of these people. Once again, the beautiful combination of wasted clubbers and worshipping dancers was united. Halfway through the night, while hanging around the edge of the dancefloor, the three of us decided to have communion – we wanted to make a physical declaration of Jesus' blood shed for everyone in the club.

A quick trip to the shop (kept open all night for ice-lollies and munchies), and we had the rather unusual combination of Ribena and Pringles for the elements. As we shared the sacrament in a most sacrilegious atmosphere, shouting the liturgy over the pounding techno music, it felt like something in the atmosphere changed. There was no large-scale visitation or physical manifestation, but from that night on I have always felt at home in Shine. While some clubs can feel oppressive or intimidating spiritually, Shine now feels warm and welcoming.

Mozambique to Miami

Through my years of clubbing, seeing some of the biggest DJs and set-ups, I began to notice that often the huge screens displaying visuals alongside the DJs don't relate to the music or add much to the overall experience. Studying computer science at the time, and desperate to avoid as much programming as possible, I managed to blag a final-year project researching colour and music, and their relationship and interdependence. Meanwhile I began learning about Video Jockeying (VJing) software, which allowed me to experiment with manipulating video clips in time with music.

This performance element is the essence of VJing – a visual art that lives and dies with the moment. In the past, from Kandinsky and the beginnings of the abstract movement, through to Fischinger and experimental film, visual artists have been limited to producing visuals which can later be viewed alongside music. VJing with a computer, however, allows the live reordering of video clips, graphics and animations that have been programmed to respond to the music. This creates the potential for a totally new experience, through a live and complementary audio-visual performance.

As I got more into it, I began to see VJing as an awesome opportunity to express my creativity and to explore a new art form, but also to communicate God's love in the nightclub environment, through incorporating scripture and prophecy into the visuals. With most clubs and venues filled with countless projectors and plasma TVs, this also meant that these messages of hope and love would be seen 30 feet wide and 20 feet high!

When I finished university in the summer of 2006, I was still excited about the possibilities open to me through VJing, but also had the ambition of one day being able to respond like Jesus did when John's disciples asked if he was the one they'd been expecting:

> Go back and tell John what you have just seen and heard:
> The blind see,
> The lame walk,
> Lepers are cleansed,
> The deaf hear,
> The dead are raised,
> The wretched of the earth
> have God's salvation hospitality extended to them.

(Luke 7.22, MSG)

That same year, 2006, I had the great privilege of attending the Iris Ministries 'School of Missions' in Pemba, Mozambique. I was there for two months, but in the very first week God fulfilled my ambition; his love literally knocked me off my feet as three deaf girls were healed. As St Paul promised in his letter to the Ephesians, God's love and power are immeasurably more than we can ask or imagine (Ephesians 3.20). I saw the blind see and the lame walk: from old men counting fingers out of eyes that had been blind just moments before, to Pastor Jone who lived in the next room to me and has raised nine people from the dead. But in among the beautiful outpouring of his love in the dusty African bush, I felt the whisper of the Spirit to go back to Miami.

I had first been to Miami two years previously with a 24-7 Prayer mission team, and had attended the Winter Music Conference – a unique gathering of global dance music culture and industry where, for five days in March each year, Miami is deluged with DJs, producers, label bosses and party people. Our initial trip there had been quite difficult, as we seemed to spend hours wandering round without any clear idea of what we should be doing. However, one night God had struck a match and showed us the treasure room through which we were walking. Two people we got chatting to were so excited to meet Christians at this event that they dropped everything and spent the whole night chatting and praying with us – one of them designed speakers for the world's biggest speaker brand, and the other was a music producer who had gone platinum 60 times. (Which means he had sold more than 60 million records!)

Despite these memories, here in Pemba, and surrounded by people dreaming of being missionaries in Africa, I struggled to keep believing in God's heart for club culture. Was God really calling me back into this culture? Or was I just imagining it? After returning from Africa, God continued to put Miami on my heart, and eventually I made up my mind to go. There wasn't much interest from the original team, but I couldn't shake the vibe so decided to take a risk and, managing to secure myself a booking to VJ at a hotel during the conference, I headed out solo to Miami.

There is a beautiful Celtic blessing for travellers which includes the line 'May the road rise up to meet you', and this is pretty much what God did in Miami. On the first day, while registering, I introduced myself to a VJ who was playing at the conference. Before I knew it, before she had even seen me play, I was offered my own stage at the 60,000-capacity music festival which would conclude the conference. I also ended up performing at the official after-party with DJing legends Goldie, and Fabio & Grooverider.

Throughout the week I had some awesome discussions about spirituality with other VJs, and had the opportunity to jam with some world-famous artists whose work had taught me a lot of what I knew. At the end of the week I was heading back to the hotel to thank God for everything, when a complete stranger struck up a conversation with me. It turned out he had designed the place, and after we'd been chatting for a while, he ended up taking me out for sushi with some others including a high-flying Microsoft web-designer. The whole week was quite ridiculous, and definitely immeasurably more than I could have asked for or imagined.

The future

Following experiences of VJing faith, hope and love in Miami, lots of doors have opened, and I've had countless opportunities to communicate God's love at art galleries and fashion shows, with bands and superstar DJs, and even at the Ministry of Sound in London. I'm still working out how to communicate better in this medium, and how to incorporate scripture in subtle yet bold ways. However, in God's grace he has given me many words to put on the screens, and revelations of his character to express in video form. I trust that he will continue to bless people through this as long as he wants to.

So where exactly does this bring us? Stories, hopes, dreams. I know Jesus is the lord of the dance, full of love and power. I have seen him move mightily in Africa, where villages have been instantly transformed. The desperate hunger of those beautiful people certainly contributes to the massive harvest and revival. But I've also seen God work miracles in the West, healing people with joy and compassion, leaving gold dust on the hands of those who worship. I am hungry for these signs and wonders in clubland; I am desperate to see revival. We're not there yet, but I still want to fight for it. Jesus put on human skin and walked around in it. He grew up in the culture of his day and poured out his love in all areas of society. Maybe a few more of us need to get addicted to bass, and find a new place in which to live out our faith.

9

Club & Pray

SARAH SMITH (LONDON)

One of my favourite Bible verses is 2 Samuel 6.14: 'David . . . danced before the Lord with all his might'. David was so fired up with passion for God that he couldn't help but express his overwhelming thanks and praise in a physical way, using every part of his body. The fact that he danced with all his might conveys a sense of total abandonment, losing all inhibitions. I can picture him really going for it, dancing with all his energy and all his heart, not caring what anyone else thought.

I can totally relate to David's desire to dance before God – and as an avid clubber, I find nightclubs the perfect setting to pray and worship. I know that might sound strange – clubs tend to be loud, murky places, packed to the brim with hundreds or thousands of sweaty people doing their thing on the dancefloor. But I love all that, there's something in the chunky, throbbing, pulsating beats that really helps me focus on God and lift up my prayers and praises to him. I love worshipping in a traditional church environment too, but dancing with all my might in a nightclub really helps me to connect with God. As though every part of my body is communicating with him.

Thankfully, I'm not the only one who is into praising God in this way. I lead a 24-7 Prayer mission team of about ten guys and gals who have a heart for the club scene in London. Once a month we go out praying and worshipping as we dance. We are from different churches across London and we started out in July 2004, responding to a call from God to bring our prayers and worship into the clubs. Basically, these are the places we would normally hang out in at the weekend anyway – so not a big hardship!

When I say we pray and worship in clubs, I don't mean that we are praying or worshipping out loud, kneeling in the middle of the dancefloor or laying hands on people in an overt way. We are simply praying and worshipping in our hearts and minds, but to onlookers we probably look like any other clubber. I know some churchgoers think it's wrong for Christians to go to nightclubs, but I think that if Jesus were living on our planet today, he would probably be out in the clubs and pubs, because that's where loads of those who need him hang out, and the Gospels show that he just loved being around people in their own social environments. Many of these people are unlikely to come to church, so it's great to try and bring a bit of church to them instead. And let's not forget it was God's idea to create music and dance in the first place!

Dancing before God

I have enjoyed clubbing for as long as I can remember. Moving to London in 1997 was a source of great excitement to me, as the clubbing opportunities were far greater than I'd been used to back home. However, it took a long time for me to feel settled in London, and it was a while before I had developed friendships with people I could go out dancing with. None of these friends were Christians, though, and they would regularly be getting drunk or high around me, but I would be right in there dancing with them, praying for them, and for other people around me. Sometimes I would pray for myself and stuff happening in my life, sometimes God would lead me to pray for other things, but mainly it would be for salvation – especially for the people around me in the clubs.

One night we were at a club called Fabric, and as I was dancing God reminded me of the testimony a young woman had given at church a few weeks before. She had been in a famous band in the early 1990s and had got caught up in the rock'n'roll lifestyle, eventually becoming addicted to heroin. She had an amazing story to tell, and it was fantastic to hear about the way God had transformed her. As I danced that night, I felt God tell me that someone had once prayed for that young woman while she was performing in a club. The person who prayed probably had no idea the impact their prayer had, but it nevertheless helped bring about a total change in her life. I felt God was really encouraging me to continue to pray for people in clubs, despite the fact that I wasn't seeing any direct results. After all, expectant prayer is powerful prayer!

Inspired to go deeper with my prayers, I started praying for a group of people dancing nearby; the atmosphere among them was very lustful and there was a spiritual heaviness in the air. As I prayed, I was getting elbowed a lot by people around me; it was particularly full that night and the jostling felt even more aggressive than usual. I was being trodden on and also got a cigarette burn on my arm. I felt as if I were in a battle, but that I was not taking any ground. Then I felt God speak to me very clearly. He said, 'You need to bring groups of people in to pray and worship.'

That makes sense, I thought. With more people praying and worshipping, maybe a greater impact could be made. However, I had been looking for Christian friends to go clubbing with for several years, yet none of the Christians I knew were into it. How was I going to find *one* person to come with me to pray and worship, let alone a whole group?

The day of small things

The next day I was at a party, and got chatting to a friend who was organizing a 24-7 Prayer week at our church in preparation for Soul in the City (a summer mission project spanning the whole of Greater London). She was looking for people to cover prayer slots over that week and, of course, the early-hour slots were tricky to fill. I suggested that I could take some people out clubbing on the Saturday night – we could be praying as we danced, and therefore cover the very early-morning slots on Sunday too. She thought it was a great idea, so the next step was to find people to join me.

I emailed some friends at church and got a great response. Loads of people thought it was a cool idea, and soon I had a team to go out with. I was very excited and encouraged. However, as Saturday night approached, team members started dropping out for various reasons – sickness, tiredness, other plans, and so on. There was only one person left, and she wasn't feeling very well either. We prayed and prayed, and thankfully she was able to come out in the end. We started the night in a temporary 24/7 prayer-room at our church, where we were sent out by a group of intercessors who prayed powerfully over both of us. The visions and words we received were very significant and affirming of what we were about to do. Then we headed out to Turnmills, one of the biggest clubs in London.

Once there, we did a quick scout around and prayed in all the rooms (including the toilets!) before heading on to the dancefloor, where we began to dance in prayer. We were very aware of God's presence around us, and he really showed us how to intercede and what to pray for. His voice tended to come in waves, and often reflected what was going on with the music – we had moments of dancing passionately where we were praying for very specific things or crying out to him, but also quieter moments trying to hear his voice, humbling ourselves and worshipping him. The words of some of the songs being spun on the decks were very pertinent. One track in particular contained the words 'reach out to me' and, as people danced with their hands in the air, there was a real sense that we were in a room full of searching souls desperate for their needs to be met. Whenever I think about this first night out, I often recall the words of Zechariah 4.10, 'Who dares despise the day of small things?' Although I was initially disappointed so many people had dropped out, leaving only two of us taking part, I nevertheless felt that God really did intend this to be a regular thing, and that being faithful to his call was more important than how many people turned up.

Preparing the way

Around this time, a friend of mine happened to mention our 'Club & Pray' vision to Phil Togwell, who heads up the 24-7 Prayer movement in the UK. Phil invited me for a coffee, and as we chatted and dreamed about the possibilities of reaching out to clubbers, he told me the club scene had been on his heart for a while, and offered me the opportunity to do the Club & Pray thing under the 24-7 Prayer banner. I didn't know all that much about 24-7 Prayer at the time, but after finding out more I jumped at the chance of having some backing and accountability. I was incredibly inspired by Phil's encouragement. When I questioned my ability to lead such a thing, he was so reassuring – especially as he viewed my lack of credentials as an asset, not a hindrance!

But this was a real stumbling block for me at the beginning. I am a shy person, and was even more shy back then. I had hoped that once I got a few people together, someone who knew what they were doing would come along and lead it properly. But God had other ideas, and continually affirmed me as a leader, paying no heed to my perplexed cries of helplessness, and instead steering me in the right direction with a knowing smile, telling me I'd been in the nest long enough and now it was time to fly.

I wrote a short article for the 24-7 Prayer website, outlining the vision for a group to go into London clubs to pray and worship, and was delighted when a number of people got in touch. The following month, four of us went to Ministry of Sound – once again we lifted our prayers and praise to Jesus, and God led our prayers as we danced together and communicated with God as a group. Over the next few months, more and more people with a passion for the club scene heard about what we were doing, and our group grew. We ended up doing a Club & Pray tour around seven of London's superclubs: Turnmills, Ministry of Sound, The End, Pacha, Heaven, Fabric, and The Cross. Each time we went we prayed and worshipped, and opened ourselves to the Holy Spirit's guidance. This often led us into conversations with other clubbers, but sometimes it was clear that prayer and worship were to be our focus.

Not by might nor by power

Another key verse for our team has been Zechariah 4.6, '"Not by might nor by power, but by my Spirit," says the Lord Almighty.' I have to admit, though, that on one occasion I blatantly bypassed the Holy Spirit bit and created my own evangelistic plan without seeking God's guidance. It was at a nightclub called The End, which was the third stop on our Club & Pray tour. I was especially keen to have conversations with fellow clubbers that night, and I got myself whipped up in an evangelistic fervour ready to convert the whole club. I approached four people separately and started talking about God as soon as possible. All four conversations fell flat on their faces, and the people I spoke to ended up thinking I was very odd.

God patiently gave me a nudge and told me to stop acting strangely, encouraging me to relax and enjoy the music and dancing. So I stepped out of my crazed evangelist shoes and stopped being such a try-hard. Later that night four other people approached me at different times, and the conversations opened up naturally so I could share something of my faith with them. It was not forced, and God was obviously at work in these situations.

As our vision developed during the Club & Pray tour, another key verse for us was Isaiah 62.10, 'Pass through, pass through the gates! Prepare the way for the people. Build up, build up the highway! Remove the stones. Raise a banner for the nations.' It increasingly seemed as if God wanted us to go into the clubs and prepare the way for him to do his thing in this culture. We were well aware that he was already at work in the clubs well before we arrived on the scene, but it was clear there was, and is, so much more to come. In going to these clubs we felt we were helping to build this highway, and in praying were helping to move the stones and obstacles out of the way.

We decided to focus on one particular club called The Cross, situated in an area of King's Cross that looks dreary, desolated and generally very sorry for itself during the day, but becomes a vibrant hub of life at night. We go to a specific club night every month, which we have been really sowing into, hoping to bump into familiar faces each time, and build relationships with the people we meet. God has continued to lead us in our prayers, and sometimes we have had clear themes for the night, such as transformation, love or forgiveness. We always pray for the resident DJ and the other DJs performing, and for the people around us on the dancefloor. We get offered pills a lot, and just saying no and explaining that we're not even drinking alcohol can be a huge witness. It can be hard for some people to understand how we have enough stamina to be out dancing until the early hours without any chemical assistance, and this can open up real opportunities for chats about our faith. One night, a member of our team had a stream of people coming up to him asking him for drugs (clearly he looked like drug dealer material!), leading to a number of opportunities to explain he is not involved with drugs, and then talk a little about his faith.

Being sure of what we hope for

Of course a club environment can be very distracting, and this sort of thing might not be for everyone. There are plenty of temptations, and keeping focused can be a real challenge, which is why we spend plenty of time in prayer before we even get to the club. We meet first to pray and worship in 24-7 Prayer's City of London prayer-room, and it's so good to get up close and personal with God before heading out to the mission field. We sometimes put Bible verses in our pockets, so if we are finding it hard to focus we can meditate on the verse while dancing or taking a break. I have also found it useful to repeat Jesus' name over and over if I'm struggling to concentrate.

Every month we also meet up on another night to keep the rhythm of prayer going when we're not clubbing. We also have meals together occasionally, and hope this will develop to the point where inviting people we meet in the clubs to have dinner with us will be a regular occurrence. We really believe that building relationships and letting people into our lives can be a fantastic witness, and may break down misconceptions they have about church and Christians. For many of those we meet, going to church is the last thing on their minds. But an invitation to dinner is much more appealing, so this will be another way of developing friendships and trust so that coming along to church with us at some point maybe won't seem so intimidating.

I would love to be able to say we have seen revival in the club scene and miracles on the dancefloor, but this is not the case. Looked at from a human perspective I could get disillusioned, but I always remember the story God told me about the woman who was prayed for and whose life was transformed, and I continue to be encouraged that people who obediently pray often have no idea what effects their prayers have. We've prayed for so many people at The Cross and all over London – for the clubbers, the DJs and the staff – and have faith that those prayers have been effective. As it says in Hebrews 11.1, 'faith is being sure of what we hope for and certain of what we do not see'. We have faith that through our prayers and conversations we have planted seeds (or watered seeds already planted), and that in this way we have contributed to many people's journeys towards Christ.

We have been privileged to witness some of these journeys up close. One night we were at a club called Heaven, and at the start of the evening we were finding it a real struggle – the place was heaving because a massive DJ (in terms of skills, not size!) called Paul van Dyk was on the decks. It was difficult for us to find room to dance, and the permeating sweatiness, combined with lack of space, was exasperating. However, things improved towards the end of the night, and we were just beginning to enjoy the music and dancing when we got chatting with a group of people dancing nearby. One of them was Mike, and as we got talking it turned out he used to go to church, but stopped going after a bad experience. He was amazed he had bumped into a group of Christians, and that they were in a club enjoying themselves! The seeds of friendship had been planted but, frustratingly, he moved to the other side of the globe shortly afterwards. Although we continued to pray for Mike, we didn't expect to see him again.

So imagine our surprise when, well over a year later, Mike got in touch to tell us he was moving back to London! He started hanging out with us, and came along clubbing a few times – and eventually he started going to church with one of our team. Mike is now back in full swing with church life and, although we'll never know how important our role was in encouraging him back into a relationship with Jesus (presumably we were just a small part of God's bigger plan), it's great to know our presence in Heaven that night had a real impact on Mike's life.

We feel so blessed that God has encouraged us in our passion for clubbing, and is using it for his glory. I'd love to encourage you to involve God in *your* passions – whether it's clubbing, DJing, going to your local pub, playing football, knitting, whatever! Maybe you should get more strategic in your socializing, and bring prayer and worship into what you love doing? You never know what might happen . . .

10
Minister of Sound

LORRAINE DIXON (BIRMINGHAM)

This time around it felt different. As a Church Army sister and Anglican priest, I have worked in various roles over the years, and coming to the end of any post is always a strange time – a period of questioning and searching, of seeking God's new direction. I had been used to parish ministry in traditional churches, but this time I felt a real sense of being called to reach out to those who didn't give a damn about Christianity, and who were indifferent or even hostile towards the church (quite possibly with good reason).

While I was mulling over this new calling, I heard that the Diocese of Birmingham was looking for someone to work with unchurched young adults aged 18–30 (the very age group that is so often missing in traditional churches). I became filled with excitement and a strong vocation to this role, which would hopefully allow me to explore what God was doing in some very surprising places. After an intensive application process, I was offered the job and, in September 2005 my husband and I relocated to Birmingham. To do what exactly, I didn't really know, but nevertheless I felt incredibly energized and optimistic about the task ahead.

This sense of euphoria didn't last long. To begin with, I was thrilled to be freed from traditional parish duties – the usual round of house visits, organizing services, preaching sermons, worrying about leaky roofs, managing church politics, and having to deal with the same people over and over again. After a month, though, I was suddenly filled with an overwhelming sense of anxiety and apprehension. I realized that having fixed points in the diary each week had previously provided me with some sense of purpose and direction and, as I began to contrast this with my new role (without any fixed boundaries of church and parish, nor regular dates in the diary), I felt very anxious and alone.

In reality I wasn't on my own in this new job – I had a line manager who met with me every few weeks, and a small steering group who met with me every few months. It was good to know they were praying with me and for me, and were at the end of a telephone whenever I needed them. Knowing how I was feeling, one member of the steering group made the practical suggestion of ensuring I had at least one regular item in my diary to help keep me rooted. So I decided to prayer-drive around my area every week, and visit key people to gather background intelligence. This helped, but my anxiety remained. I often found myself suffering migraines and regularly took to my bed with headaches and nausea.

I still felt incredibly alone in this experimental post – but because of this, I found all I could do was rely on God, and depend on him to see me through. Over the following weeks and months, my prayer life became more intense than ever before, and my prayers came alive as a real dialogue with our God who loves us and never gives up on us. As I journeyed on with God, it occurred to me why I had been given such a strong calling to this post – for times like this, when doubt and fears assailed me and I felt like giving up. This calling gave me the strength to not give in to the very real temptation to leave it all behind.

Do not be afraid

For years now I have kept a journal, in which I record my thoughts and prayers and the things I feel God is saying to me. Looking back through these journals as I piece together my story, I am reminded that, throughout this long dark night of the soul, I consistently heard God whispering the words of Isaiah 43.5 into my spirit: 'Do not be afraid, for I am with you.' Disheartened as I was, the journey continued, and I knew God was accompanying me every step of the way.

Wednesday 12 October 2005

Take nothing for the journey, for I go with you. I am your rock and your shield. Stay with me, remain with me, that is all I ask. I will bless you in all you do for me. Go and make disciples. Do not doubt your purpose and do not doubt your gifts, your JOY and my PEACE. Just take it one step at a time – a little here, a little there, it all adds up. Focus on me. Do not worry, my precious, I know it is difficult.

The task may have loomed enormous before me, but I was being daily encouraged by God. But, as I didn't have the usual parish 'roadmap' to tell me what to do, I was faced with the question 'Where do I start?' I decided the priority was getting to know my patch, so I continued driving around my area, stopping at different points, observing what was going on, praying, seeking God, finding out where the young adults were, and where they tended to spend their time. The headaches, sickness and anxiety continued to stalk me, and this continued to have a corresponding effect on my prayers. I remember well the day I felt desperate and got angry with God, asking why he had called me to Birmingham and why I was in this truly mad job. I asked him for a sign I was really needed there, or reassurance that I would be able, in any shape or form, to explore what a Jesus-centred community might look like for young adults in this area. Finally, I ended with the threat that I would leave this seemingly pointless post if I didn't get an answer!

The next day, God had mercy on me. I was prayer-driving around the area when I heard a still, small voice say, 'Do not fret or worry, my child. Just go, and I'll mark out your steps.' This reassurance was followed by an unexpected revelation about what could be – and at that very moment I had the idea of hosting club nights in the city, following the trail of young adults from the suburbs to the city centre, where they spent most of their leisure time. It occurred to me that at such nights, the music and the vibe could speak of kingdom values, putting the love of God at the centre of the activities, opening people up to a sense of the divine. I was so overwhelmed I had to stop the car and park by the side of the road. I had been on the brink of despair, but God met me in my need, and gifted me with great joy and peace – a joy and peace I was to share in the clubs. I immediately rang a friend to ask his advice about this insight. He felt it was right, as did my line manager and steering group, who blessed this new direction and who have continued to have great faith in this vision.

Sunday 27 November 2005

Don't forget, you have a great capacity for love and joy, my gifts to you, to help you in your way forward. You are my gift to the community, not because you are perfect, but because you are set apart to do my will. Image this, Lorraine. Show my people who are lost and searching that I love them and I am here – for they know already but may be confused. Yes, my child, you have a great gift for joy and laughter. Use it to bring my people home. Such joy has come from sad places for you, so share my compassion, for that is my gift to you also. Do not be afraid, for I am with you. I have called you by name and you are mine.

My purpose was now clear. There hadn't been any flashes of light or the sudden miracle of an instant community, but God had provided me with a glimpse of what could be, and that was enough to help me move forward in faith. Over the coming weeks God enabled me to cross paths with various key people from the dance community – I would pop into record stores and unexpectedly meet DJs, promoters or clubbers, all of whom helped me develop a better picture of the local club scene. Very few were Christians, but they somehow understood what I was about, and were very supportive. I decided to professionalize my skills as a DJ and, shortly afterwards, an important DJ conference organized by Birmingham-based Punch Records provided me with countless further networking opportunities. I also started going to various club nights in town, and began to meet people there. Overall, God seemed to be confirming this path.

Bringing joy to the house

A few years earlier I'd met a group of young women from Liberia who had given me the name 'Ayodele' – meaning 'brings joy to the house'. This seemed to be a prophetic choice and, shortening it to Ayo, meaning joy, I embraced this in my new identity as DJ Ayo (pronounced *eye-oh*). This name acknowledges both my African roots and the joy I feel in being a God-seeker, a Christ-follower and a Spirit-lover.

Thursday 8 December 2005

Yes. Lord, in your grace and mercy you gave me insight into your purpose for me – to be stamped with the Spirit and to image Christ in our world through gospel club nights and DJing. Praise God! All my experiences have led to this moment. My heart is so full of joy . . . God's response seemed to be: My child, I didn't want to put you in a cage, but for you to use the gifts I've given you – your joy and your faith in me. These I wish you to share, keeping it real, joyful, and extremely funky.

I wasn't new to the dance scene, as over the years I'd been invited to play the records at countless parties, but I had never considered myself a DJ. However, when I attended the DJ Academy early in 2006 (where I learnt about setting up the equipment, mixing, scratching, promotions, and even how to DJ properly with two turntables) I realized that this was pretty much what I'd been doing all along. No wonder God placed this call upon my heart! God will often use our passions to answer his call on our lives, enabling us to be truly ourselves as we engage in his mission. In my case, these passions included a love of house music, clubbing and dance culture. My hope was to use this love to create common ground with young adults who were also into this, and thus make connections in a genuine way. As I journeyed into the club scene, I was consistently encouraged by the words of Philippians 2.15–16 (MSG): 'Provide people with a glimpse of good living and of the living God. Carry the light-giving Message into the night.'

New beginnings

At the beginning of 2006 we launched the new project at my commissioning service, held at a shopping mall on my patch. The service was informal and creative, and I ended the evening with my first professional set as DJ Ayo. Over 150 people turned up for the service (a wonderful mixture of people from the local churches and people I'd met in the club scene), and as an added bonus various passers-by popped in to see what was going on. Afterwards, one of the outlets at the mall invited me to host an event that Easter, for which I invited a number of singers and MCs to perform alongside me as I spun the records. This was a pattern we maintained at other club nights we hosted throughout the year, at various venues in and around the city centre. A one-off event at a bar in Digbeth led to a midweek residency which continued for the rest of the year, enabling me to establish a real sense of being a priestly presence in such places. Whenever I DJed, I would wear my dog collar, and would regularly be asked if I was a vicar. Despite the initial incredulity when I told them I was, this consistently provided openings for conversations about music, life, mad stuff, deep stuff, and God. Some people asked for prayer for their families, their friends or themselves, and one woman even asked me to bless her new crucifix. I felt incredibly privileged to be there and to share in the lives of these young adults. They even nicknamed me 'The Vicar of Digbeth'!

Saturday 25 February 2006

'I am confident of this, that the one who began a good work among you will bring it to completion by the day of Jesus Christ' (Philippians 1.6, NRSV). Take this as an encouragement about your new ministry. Be assured I am with you, my child. Do not be afraid. Be encouraged about what has been started, and continue in my name. I bless you my child.

After a while, we decided to bring the various club nights and events under the banner of 'Taste & See the Light' promotions (taking our name from Psalm 34.8). At Taste & See events, we play deep soulful dance music, which speaks of faith, hope, peace and love – to nourish the spirit and move the soul. We do not believe God is contained in one form of music, but can be encountered in all sorts of genres, so we try to keep the music eclectic, although usually with an emphasis on soulful tunes, driving tribal rhythms, and funky phat basslines to move the body and lift the soul. Here people can dance, get caught up in the music, put their hands in the air, and perhaps connect with the Divine Funky One. For we believe that God is creative and funky, and can be met and encountered in the groove, as well as worshipped and praised in the dance (Psalm 149.3).

For me, the name 'Taste & See the Light' emphasizes the invitation we offer for people to explore the possibilities of God. At our events we don't try to get people along to a church, but instead encourage them to *be* church, or a community of seekers, where they are. It is clear that many people, particularly young adults, are turned off by traditional church services, which can appear dull and locked into habits of inaccessible religiosity. We sense that now is the time to follow God into new places where we can explore new shapes of church, new experiences of being pilgrims on a spiritual journey, new wineskins for a new generation. We want to utilize bar/club culture to develop space where people can gather to find love, friendship, hope and meaning, all shaped by a Christ-centred spirituality. For many, the bar or club is their church. Several years ago, the band Faithless expressed this in their song 'God is a DJ', which pointed to the deep sense of connection, even healing, that many feel as they dance together. Taste & See is about inviting people to put a toe in the water, to explore the possibility that God runs to meet us in our funky, sweaty, sensual humanity – as we are and where we are.

Our dream is that a real community will grow out of the events we host, but until then it's all about people coming along and feeling that this is a warm and open space. Through these gatherings, we hope to meet the needs of people who long for an encounter with God in a new way, without alienating those who describe themselves as non-religious. We endeavour to make the vibes friendly and joyful – for we are all one people under the groove. Everyone is welcome and will be made welcome. Just taste and see!

Through it all

God had given me a break, but I still faced many difficulties. In particular, I had to contend with opposition from people in the wider church who didn't like what I was doing – some of them even called the project a betrayal of the gospel! Others asked why we didn't just play gospel music and make it a Christian club event. I explained that the particular path I was on was the one where I felt God had placed me, and that I had to stay faithful to God's call on my life to go into the night and be the light.

I was also struggling with the fact that we often had relatively low numbers of people coming to our events. The reality is, unless you have sufficient sponsorship to book a big-name live act or a superstar DJ, new promoters on the dance scene will inevitably struggle when starting out. I had a limited budget and had to make do with myself and various local acts. Even though I knew it would be slow going at the outset, sometimes it still felt as if I was facing an insurmountable challenge – as if I was hitting my head against a brick wall.

Wednesday 29 March 2006

Lord, you'll need to help me, it seems such a huge task . . . I sensed God's reply: Do not fret, I am with you. I love you and I need you to do this. Stick with it, my child. Taste & See will take time, as the task is a hard one. But hopefully joyful too. Stick with the music, and think on me.

On top of all this, there was still the overwhelming sense of being alone. Despite the steering group, despite the very real help from my husband and the support of family and friends, and despite God being very present along the way – I still felt on my own in this post. I realized that what I really needed was a 'core group' who would consistently pray with me and for the project, as well as come along to the club nights.

Thursday 3 August 2006

I've been feeling very alone and down these past few days, and tired too. I still can't find anyone to depend on. Why? Every time I think, 'Yes I have a core group member', something happens and they let me down. Can't I have anyone to work with? Am I cursed to be alone? I need a team, I need this particularly for those days I feel alone. I need you to come through for me, Lord, I need you to hear my plea and help me!

This sense of aloneness remained with me for the rest of the year, but God was there with me in the midst of my desperation, providing comfort, support and guidance throughout. He continued to bless me with an unexpected yet very real joy, enabling me to keep on in faith despite the many knocks I experienced. However, as we turned the corner into 2007, I finally found five core group members to accompany me on this strange journey. We regularly meet for prayer over lunch or dinner, sometimes I send them text messages with prayer requests, and whenever possible they come to my events – to pray, chat, dance, interact, and generally be cool human beings. At last I felt I was no longer alone in the work!

Encountering God in House

By the beginning of 2007, I had become friends with a number of local DJs who started asking me to DJ at their nights, and who, in turn, I was able to call on to play at mine. Around this time we developed a new club night called 'Love Joy', where I began to collaborate with a couple of local DJs in particular – Lee Hills (a fellow DJing minister in the Diocese of Birmingham) and Damien Deighan (a tutor at the DJ Academy), who were very sympathetic towards the project's aims. We were fortunate in finding a venue that was intimate and funky, and where the bar-staff and bouncers were extremely welcoming – which meant it was perfect for the joyful vibe we wanted to encourage. Love Joy soon became the main thrust of Taste & See promotions, with a focus on encountering God in House and seeking God in the groove. Love Joy is a real attempt to draw close to urban young adults who are far beyond the church walls, and to offer a joyful space speaking of kingdom values and of the God who loves unconditionally. Our only strategy is authentic relationships, and the project travels at the pace of those relationships.

Wednesday 21 February 2007

Just focus on me and on my will for your life – to be in this place, at this time, at this moment. To be light in the night, and to image my joy and love to the joyless and the loveless.

Around this time, I also starting thinking about the opportunities radio could provide in reaching out to the dance community in Birmingham – and as my friendship with Damien Deighan grew, we talked about the possibility of doing a radio show together. Damien already had radio experience, and I was doing some training at the local black community radio station, Newstyle Radio 98.7 FM. We presented the station managers with a demo for a show in which we would play upfront and classic soul, deep house, and soulful house, and they immediately offered us a slot on Saturday nights! The first edition of our show *Soulfood* went out in the summer of 2007, and is still going strong.

Seeking God in the groove

Meanwhile, Lee Hills and I started talking about exploring worship through dance music. I told Lee about my vision for hosting something in my home that would bring together the various strands of my being a disciple of Christ, DJ, priest and clubber. In turn, Lee told me about Groove Fellowships (an idea he'd seen on www. tastyfresh.com, a website dedicated to encouraging and connecting Christians in the dance scene). The aim of these fellowships is to be a space where people involved in club culture can get together regularly for worship, support, music, food and networking.

Out of these conversations, 'Revive: Seeking God in the Groove' was born. We host these monthly gatherings in our homes, where there is a warm welcome, food and dance music as people arrive, followed by DJ-led worship, during which one of us DJs, and the other MCs some words of worship on the microphone. People are encouraged to join in, dance, or simply sit back and relax. As the worship comes to a climax, the music gets more uptempo, and we finish up with people chilling out, chatting or dancing. There are usually a dozen or so at these Revive sessions, and they tend to be those who, like us, are lovers of the club scene. We like to describe Revive as both a journey and an opportunity to meet with God. The journey, which is ongoing, is about learning to worship God using dance music, as well as in and through club culture. And, of course, it's also about inviting others to journey with us.

Monday 12 March 2008

Keep searching, keep looking for my lost sheep, for those travellers seeking a way home. Keep searching, keep looking, keep being light in the night, that is all I ask. Keep searching. Keep looking.

So where are we now? Well, it's been a couple of years since the commissioning service, and over this time my role has changed and developed; I am now more focused on exploring different ways of doing and being church that might appeal to people like me, who find it easier to connect with the Big G through dance music than through *Songs of Praise*! After many years of conducting Sunday services, weddings and christenings as a parish priest, somehow I have now become a club promoter and a DJing vicar, or 'minister of sound'. Other days the path I'm walking seems completely crazy, although it is almost always a joy. Some days I still lose confidence in what we're trying to do – but the call of God and the support of those around me enable me to keep on. I look forward to the ongoing journey, and look with expectancy to the discoveries and surprises that will inevitably crop up along the way!

11
From Gorillas to Disciples

DAVE CATES (SHEFFIELD)

Sheffield. The UK's fifth largest city and home to some of the most successful British bands and clubs – Arctic Monkeys, Pulp, ABC, Róisín Murphy, The Tuesday Club, Urban Gorilla, and Gatecrasher, to name just a few. A city that achieved worldwide fame for its steel industry, and is currently home to two universities, the largest college in Europe, and over 50,000 students. A city with one of the most deprived districts in Europe, but also with the country's most affluent area outside London. A city with a population of well over 600,000 people, but with only around 2 per cent of these people regularly attending church.

Welcome. This is our city and our home. A modern multi-cultural urban community, a major city with a village feel, which for many years played host to our attempts to realize a clubbers' church. When I look around the country, I get excited by all the new churches springing up – excited not just because they are helping people see Jesus rather than religion, but also because it seems that the fear of failure is rapidly deteriorating. For anyone familiar with the history of the Nine O'clock Service (one of the first groups to seriously attempt to make connections between church and rave culture in the late 80s and early 90s), the idea of a clubbers' church in

Sheffield is no new thing. However, lacking proper accountability, and with a manipulative and dictatorial leadership, the Nine O'clock Service eventually crashed and burned. But, despite all the mistakes made, I believe the original vision was spot on with God's heart, and that the positive lessons learnt are still an amazing inspiration for our creative Christian communities today, as we attempt to innovatively establish a relevant, effective and living church in our current cultural setting.

In the late 90s, I was the leader of a small mission-focused community called d3, through which we aimed to love, serve and make disciples within the Sheffield club scene. This was a mission community attached to St Thomas' Church, which was, at the time, meeting in the famous Roxy nightclub, and was an awesome church for many of us to call home – but the d3 community also involved people from a wide range of Sheffield churches. Together we worshipped God, explored the nature of church, went clubbing, took to the streets, and supported one another as best we could as we looked to see a culture transformed. We were not trying to create some sort of 'attractional' church; we were simply a community of Christians who loved going clubbing, and desperately wanted to introduce our clubbing mates to Jesus. We were involved in a wide range of projects, such as running club nights, taking teams on mission trips to Ayia Napa and Ibiza, partnering with 24-7 Prayer in running prayer-rooms, and leading club-style worship at churches and conferences. Despite all these amazing adventures, I am convinced that the areas that had the greatest and most lasting impact were the shared life of the community and our long-term presence in the clubs.

Making disciples

Making disciples was Jesus' command to us, not building the church – he said that he'll build the church, and that we're to make disciples. Having this principle as the basis of mission can radically transform the whole concept of increasing the size of our Christian community. Over the years I have worked alongside a number of different churches and ministries, and this one single concept very often blows them away. It may seem like such a simple change of thinking, but it can lead to a complete shift of perspective and priorities.

Let me ask you a question: When you look at our town centres at night, at clubbers, at people falling out of clubs and bars in the small hours, at drunks fighting on the streets, at the proliferation of casual sexual experiences, what do you think first: 'Man, how much these people need church' or 'God, how much these people need Jesus'?

So 98 per cent of people in Sheffield don't go to church. So what? How many people *know* Christ? How many have had a *revelation* of God? These are the questions that really count. Talking to people in the clubs and on the streets reveals the fact that a huge number of people believe in God, and some have even had experiences of God (or some higher power) speaking to them. I'm sure Satan loves spreading fear and lies about how few people are open to hearing about Jesus – but in my experience it's all about how you relate Jesus to them. A pilled-up clubber needs a Jesus who unleashes the ultimate highs, the craziest healings, and the biggest buzz from seeing people fixed up. Just as a girl trapped in prostitution needs a Jesus who shows unconditional love, heals, restores and offers sacrificial love with no strings attached. Just as a middle-class office worker needs to know there's a spontaneous and exciting Jesus who shows there's more to life than spreadsheets, statistics, grey suits, taxes, a mortgage, a carefully planned pension scheme, and then . . . what?

To each and every one of us, Jesus reveals himself in a different way. It's a relationship. This is how we disciple others – by inviting them into this relationship, by helping them meet the Jesus we love but, more importantly, who loves them.

Being church

At the core of our attempts to engage with club culture was our community of Christian clubbers. Within d3, our aim was to be a proper expression of church within club culture, a community of like-minded Christians trying our best to live as Jesus did, in the world but not of it, walking a hardcore, uncompromised lifestyle, and constantly reaching out to the culture we belong to and are called to – meeting people, discipling them on their turf, and welcoming them into our community. Our mission statement was simple:

> To be a fully functioning cultural interface between God and club culture, by showing people within club culture the gospel in a truly accessible format, by helping bring them into a relationship with their Saviour, while providing a community within which they can belong.

The first step was to build our community to the point where we could be confident we were all fully engaging with the plans and desires God had for our lives. It doesn't take a genius to work out that actively seeking God's kingdom within clubland is going to result in Satan trying to batter you! (I think we can so often blind ourselves to the reality that, even though Jesus has beaten Satan, it's still a battle out there and we may see casualties. I'm not saying Jesus won't fight for us or that we won't see victory, but we need to be aware of the spiritual reality surrounding us.)

Worshipping together once a week in small groups, using dance music as the backdrop, and with each of us empowered to bring God's word into the mix, along with lots of prayer and prophecy – we tried to live out church as people in and of a culture, but not dictated by it. We worshipped using dance, hip-hop, punk, metal and pop music (secular and Christian). We used video visuals, everyday objects, and anything else we could creatively apply to enhance our worship context. We didn't follow any liturgy or dogmatic traditions, but if it all comes from a relationship with Jesus and a love of the Bible, then it's fine by me! Church was not just a meeting of friends at someone's house – it was everything we did, it was everywhere we were.

One element of our community life that I still get a buzz from is the fact that some of our most powerful worshipping moments were actually in the clubs. I remember one night at Gatecrasher, where we danced, prayed and worshipped to a soundtrack of the most amazing trance tunes as Paul Van Dyk led us through a seven-hour spiritual journey. Then at 6am we went outside and joined the other half of the d3 team in handing out chocolate bars and bottles of water as the 'crasher kids' spilled out into the freshly dawning Sunday morning. Sarah was part of this little community, and the dancefloor of her favourite club was where she found God's holy place:

The thing I loved most about going clubbing with a focus on worshipping Jesus, and on looking for opportunities to demonstrate his love, was the freedom we felt and the way that this attracted people. Sometimes conversations would start up in the queues or with the bouncers before we even got inside the club. Once inside, we wouldn't drink but would just hit the dancefloor and start worshipping God – to begin with, it would sometimes feel awkward, but then the joy would rise up inside me and I wouldn't be able to stop myself from jumping all around and really going for it! The music helped lead us into worship and, with the beats leading everyone into a state of euphoria, we would be there in their midst with our arms in the air, worshipping God and praying for the people all around us.

As we danced, people would come up to us and ask us what we were so happy about, if we'd taken anything, or invite us to come and dance with them. As soon as we got chatting, we would tell them we were worshipping Jesus, or we were in the club praying, or ask them if they believed in Jesus. This would either lead to an abrupt end to the conversation (if it turned out the guy was just trying to pull), or it would often lead to a long chat about life, God, spiritual experiences, and all sorts. After a while, people began to recognize us and knew we would be praying in the club. People would often ask us to pray for them or for their friends and relatives, and some of them came along to church to find out more.

Reaching out

The call to mission is central to our understanding of faith, but in my experience there's an ongoing tension between 'social action' and the more direct 'preaching the good news' approach. Sometimes I can see the value in the 'serving people' kind of mission (helping people out, offering bottles of water and bars of chocolate outside clubs, getting people into taxis or home safely, and so on), but I can't help grappling with the question 'Is this making disciples?' Sure, Jesus cared for and healed people, but a challenge or word about their eternal state of affairs was never far away. To me, if you're just handing out bottles of water, but not also telling people about Jesus and his love for them, then it's simply not evangelism – aren't you just handing out bottles of water?

We've been involved in both these approaches in Sheffield – the 'serving' type and the more upfront 'talking to people directly about Jesus' type. Both are great but usually have differing outcomes, and often different purposes. Sometimes it's appropriate simply to put the Christian community on the map by serving and witnessing, but sometimes it's time to put yourself out there and let God lead you to people, so you can talk to them about Jesus and his desire for their lives – or, even better, so you can let God give you prophetic insight into their lives and a direct word for that moment and pray for them.

That said, some of the most memorable and fruitful times we've had have been when we've combined both approaches. I remember one Friday night when we gathered together for an hour or so of prayer and worship, followed by an inspirational talk, before setting out for the busiest street in Sheffield city centre. About 40 of us went out that night, offering water and chocolate to clubbers we met, getting into countless conversations about Jesus, and seeing numerous people asking for prayer.

An experience like this, with so many involved, may sound amazing – but I just keep looking at the size of our city and thinking we still have a massive way to go. So, alongside these more extrovert forms of mission we also tackled making disciples within specific clubbing communities. Discipleship is a process, not an event – and I am convinced the pursuit of the 'event' has been one of the biggest distractions of the church in recent times. There have been some great events leading to some amazing things happening, but if all those massive stadiums were full of non-believers who became Christians, where would they all go? How would our churches cope? If we really want to see revival break out and the city come into our believing community, surely we need a structure or strategy that can cope with it. We all want to see the kingdom come on earth as in heaven, but have we truly processed what this would look like?

Discipling people within their communities is a very manageable way of growing the church. Why have we got such an obsession with having everyone under one roof? Why does the size of a single congregation matter? Within the club scene, there are already good, even amazing communities of clubbers already in existence. If they were to be discipled (and then to disciple others) within their own communities, the load on the 'traditional' or 'established' church would decrease, while simultaneously the possibilities for growth would dramatically increase! But how do you bring about this form of church? How does an existing non-Christian community become a church? The answer is simple – just as Acts tells us, we need to find the key leader in that community. If that leader extends grace towards you and becomes a Christian, then it's only a matter of time before the whole community will be influenced by that leader's new faith, and hopefully many others will find Jesus too.

Several years ago I was inspired by the suggestion that when we approach discipleship the order should be 'belonging, believing, behaving'. The idea is that people should feel they *belong* to, and are accepted by, the church community from the very outset – which may be some time before they *believe* in Jesus (if ever), and will almost certainly be a long time before a change of *behaviour* comes out of this life-changing relationship with Jesus. After all, Jesus didn't come to earth to lay down the law, but because he wanted people to be fixed up and made well – to change their broken, messed-up ways of living into transformed lifestyles. Not because of the law, but because of *love* – because he always wants what's best for us.

Taking this 'belonging, believing, behaving' approach means that someone who struggles with alcoholism, for example, can still drink while being accepted as part of our church community. Our hope is that when that person experiences Jesus' power and healing, it's then they'll have the strength to overcome the addiction – if God doesn't heal them first! This process is especially effective when they are surrounded by a supportive community to help and encourage them. Discipleship often starts just as those three words – belonging, believing, behaving – suggest, just as it did when Jesus was training up the original disciples. And I find it truly encouraging to think that most of them only got past the 'belonging' stage after Jesus had ascended into heaven!

Being consistent

Within d3 community we tried to demonstrate the love of God to non-Christian clubbers in an accessible way, and to provide a space where they could belong, learn about Jesus, and be nurtured – spiritually, physically, mentally and emotionally. We also hoped to be an example and role model within the club scene, creating a safe environment for people to enjoy the clubbing experience without feeling compromised, abused or threatened. For some, such as Kate, d3 was the first Christian community they belonged to. Here Kate tells a little of her story:

Urban Gorilla is a club night that plays dance, trance and breaks music. It attracts people mainly in their twenties and thirties, and the scene is very much a drug culture, especially for those who are middle class with stressful jobs. On our first night at Urban Gorilla as a team, we spent almost the whole evening dancing and worshipping Jesus. As the night came to an end, Catherine and I got chatting to some of the bouncers. They joked around with us at first, and then we asked one of them whether there was anything he wanted prayer for. The others laughed, but none the less he admitted that he was interested and that he wanted to talk about it some more. He asked us all sorts of questions – What is prayer? How do you pray? Did we pray five times a day towards Mecca? Do you need to be quiet to pray? What kind of things do we need to pray for?

We told him about Jesus and shared some of our own experiences of prayer, then after a while this lad with a big orange cross on his T-shirt turned up and joined in the conversation. The bouncer ended up asking us to pray for his migraines (which would sometimes get so bad he couldn't work for weeks) and for his dad (who was a depressive alcoholic). Eventually we said goodbye to the bouncer, but carried on chatting to the lad with the orange cross. He explained that he was a Christian and had been coming to Urban Gorilla with his sister for months. They had been praying that they'd meet other Christians to reach the club with, and in particular that they'd get an opportunity to speak to this very bouncer, who turned out to be head of security for several local clubs!

Another night I went to sit down for a rest after a good long session worshipping on the dancefloor, when a guy came and sat next to me. To begin with I wasn't sure whether to talk to him, because I didn't want to come across as chatting him up – after all, the reason I was there was to tell people the good news and to love them. In the end I decided to get straight to the point, so I leaned over and asked him whether he believed in Jesus. He looked confused and asked me to repeat what I had just said. I asked him again, 'Do you believe in Jesus?' He was naturally quite surprised by my question, but he was intrigued and we got chatting. Over the coming weeks he regularly came back and asked what God was speaking to me about. After a few weeks, it got to where he would open up to us about all sorts of situations occurring in his life – he said he felt good about himself after chatting with us (we would tell him this was the Holy Spirit at work), and he just seemed so amazed that we were interested and willing to listen.

In fact, he was so amazed that he went back home and told all his friends. The following week he brought along a friend (who doesn't normally go clubbing) just so that he could talk to us. The week after this he brought along a few more friends. Week after week we would sit and chat with them in the chill-out area of the club. It got to the point where we had a queue of his friends waiting to talk to us about the mess and mayhem going on in their lives – family issues, problems with drugs and alcohol, relationships, work, anything and everything. Sometimes we would just listen, sometimes we were able to bring the conversation round to Jesus, sometimes we would pray with them, and one week the original guy asks about the Bible – so I whip out my copy and we end up reading one of the stories together and talking about what it meant. This was a real answer to prayer. The following week he told me he'd been reading the Bible on the internet with an online study guide. A few weeks later he told me he'd seen a homeless man struggling with a number of heavy bags and offered to help him, and ended up chatting to him for hours. He said that he didn't normally do that kind of thing – the Holy Spirit was clearly at work in his life!

Knowing when to move on

In spite of our wonderful adventures with God in the club scene, we eventually realized it was time to disband d3. We'd had a good run at it, and over our six years we'd seen about 40 people move through the group, with a core of around a dozen at any one time. We'd seen de-churched people discover a relevant, exciting and authentic church community that manifested Jesus in ways they'd never experienced before. We'd seen un-churched people show a willingness to be prayed for, and we'd seen them experience physical, emotional and spiritual healing as a result. To top it all off, we'd seen some of them discovering Jesus. We'd also witnessed amazing, even miraculous, transformations in our own lives. But by 2005, personal circumstances were changing for many of us, and we decided to reassess where we were going as a community. After all, the world around us never stands still, and neither does God – so why should we?

My own big change was that I was getting married. In a society full of broken marriages and fractured relationships, a successful and fulfilling marriage can be an incredibly powerful witness, so as a couple we felt we needed to spend the first two years simply working out how to be married. Therefore we decided to step down from any leadership roles or anything else that might distract us from building our marriage on the right foundations. However, this change didn't necessarily mean the end of d3, as throughout our time as a mission-community one of my core leadership aims had been to raise up leaders – not just people with delegated leadership tasks, but leaders who could eventually take over my role or pursue their own vision. As I began the process of stepping down, it occurred to me that our community consisted almost entirely of potential leaders – and with that realization came the feeling that many of them were also ready to move on, and take the lead in new adventures. Around this time our mother church had begun to plant small mission-communities into some of Sheffield's inner-city estates, and as we sought God's direction for the future of d3 it became clear that several of our community should investigate joining these inner-city church plants.

Meanwhile, the group of girls that had been committed to going to Urban Gorilla every week still had their hearts set on seeing God's kingdom reign in their club, and so they continued for a while after the rest of us moved on. Together they had seen significant fruit growing from their consistent presence in the club, had built some good relationships with the regulars, seen healing and transformation, and were beginning to see Jesus grow in people's lives. However, their whole team was female, and they began to feel they needed some male support in the club. After months of praying, they decided it was time to lay out a fleece and see whether God would provide the much-needed male team-members. But they didn't materialize, and so the girls eventually took the step of faith to call it a day.

Sometimes God speaks in such practical ways. It may not be what we want to hear, but we have to trust that God knows best. When I look at all the different people who moved through the d3 community, and see the fruit of God in their lives today, I get so excited. Almost all of them are still actively involved in mission-communities throughout Sheffield or wherever they are now, putting into practice the lessons we learnt from our time together in d3. Looking back, I know with absolute certainty that God had his hand over the whole life of our community, on each and every one of us, and on the plans he had for our future.

That's another great thing about focusing on making disciples rather than building the church – when people feel it's time to move on, they can. There are no huge overheads, no bills to pay, and very few practical obligations. We're all free and able to move wherever and whenever God prompts us. This excites me so much – the idea of people following God's lead and making disciples wherever they find themselves. If the original ministry dies for whatever reason, so what? Let it die. Move on. Jesus said *he'll* build the church – our role is simply to make disciples.

12

Talking Space

GREG BARTLEM (COVENTRY)

The Skydome is a bustling commercial complex in the heart of Coventry city centre. It houses a cinema, ice-rink and three night-clubs, with several pubs and bars nearby. In recent years, the city centre has increasingly seen trouble flare as people leave the Skydome, and the following morning the surrounding area bears the scars of the night before, with broken bottles and discarded fast-food wrappers littering the streets, and untold damage done to local buildings and property.

Quite bizarrely, this ultra-modern arena was built immediately next door to the Spon Street Conservation Area, home to the city's medieval shopping street and the ancient Church of St John the Baptist. With the old so close to the new, the contrasts are obvious: the church all locked up at night with the nearby nightlife bursting at its seams, thousands of clubbers milling past the church every night, oblivious to its presence. This is the story of how we attempted to enter the Coventry club scene, and re-engage with the community around us.

The story begins

For the last few years I've been Youth Officer for the Anglican Diocese of Coventry, working to help church congregations build links with young people who gather outside the walls of their church buildings. I do this mainly through recruiting and training teams of volunteers, then going out with them on to the streets as we try to initiate and sustain relationships with local gangs of teenagers. We offer prayer and assistance (and chocolates) to any who are in trouble and, as friendships deepen, we swap the chocolates for chips and say grace over these shared meals – which sometimes provokes conversations about God. Ultimately the goal is to create worship-ful communities within youth culture.

In 2004, Roger Morris was appointed Director of Parish Development and Evangelism for the diocese, and one of the first things that drew me to him was his ability to understand the 'cringe factor' in so much of church outreach. (Neither of us are fans of aggressive 'Make way!' approaches to evangelism!) A few months later, Roger and I went for a drink with Keith Parr, the Cathedral Youth Minister, and ended up talking about the Coventry nightlife. Roger told us about a night he had recently spent in a police van patrolling the streets of Coventry, and the mayhem he'd witnessed in the small hours of the morning.

Roger is a natural pioneer who has a passion for finding original ways of taking the gospel to unreached people groups, and it soon became clear he was driving the conversation towards the idea of us attempting to engage with club culture. This seemed like a great idea but, as I saw it, we faced a major problem – our age! All of us were in our late thirties, and long past our clubbing prime. It took some persuading, but eventually Keith and I reluctantly agreed to pay a visit to the Skydome at night, to check out how we might get involved.

A few weeks later, the three of us met up on a Friday evening and made our way into the city centre. Over a game of pool, Roger told us that he'd heard about nightclub chaplaincy schemes in various towns and cities all over the UK. This sounded really exciting, and suddenly I pictured myself engrossed in deep and meaningful con-versations with clubbers, while all around people danced and drank themselves into oblivion. 'How difficult can this actually be?' I asked myself. I was soon to find out.

As the night wore on, the three of us moved on to a nearby club, where the music rated high on the cheese factor, and where everyone seemed up for a good time. The three of us endeavoured to chat with people, but the trouble was it was all so loud – a particular problem for me, due to my partial deafness (the consequence of a misspent youth). All told, I simply felt too old for this kind of work! A few hours later I came out of the club feeling dejected – clubbing ministry was evidently not for me. As we left, however, the three of us watched as people spilled out of the clubs. We witnessed a cauldron of emotions and arguments erupt, fights kick off, and even scantily clad girls walking home alone in tears. In the midst of this we asked, 'God, where are you in all this?'

A couple of days later we hatched a plan. The idea was to provide a space in the churchyard of St John's where people could stop, sit down, get a hot drink and find someone who would listen to their stories – to their hopes and dreams, their problems and fears. In a world where everyone wants to sell something, our hope was that by simply offering to listen, we would be able to communicate to those who came along that they are worth listening to. Soon, we had gathered together Christians from several city centre churches, and launched 'Talking Space', a ministry to clubbers.

Talking Space

Talking Space runs every Friday night between midnight and 4am, with a team of around five volunteers. Each week a team leader collects a radio from the city centre night wardens, then begins the evening with a short prayer and briefing session where the team leader can bring the team up to speed with what's been going on during the last few weeks, and relay up-to-the-moment information from the night wardens. Tables, chairs and outdoor heaters are then set out around a gazebo while we begin to brew hot drinks, and by 12.30am we're ready for our first 'customers'.

Normally we start with the 'flower ladies'. These are Filipino women who come to the cities in the UK looking for work, and end up working all hours, desperately trying to make ends meet by selling roses to budding Romeos. We try to make a big fuss of our flower ladies, as they tend to get treated like dirt by clubbers. We take hot drinks out to them and have a chat. (Although we always invite them back to our little hideout in the churchyard, for some reason they never come.)

After the flower ladies come the homeless, and the borderline homeless. We have found that Talking Space provides a real sanctuary for these people, keeping them safe from the sort of vicious drinkers who always seem ready to 'put the boot in'. I will never forget the night from those early days when we encountered a cold, shivering lad who had thrown himself into an ornamental fountain simply to retrieve a small handful of coins that passers-by had tossed in for good luck. Sadly, we were unable to provide an immediate solution to this lad's material needs, other than offering him a sleeping bag as some respite from the cold. However, I hope that the kindness he experienced, and the simple offer of having his story heard, will have been of some small help.

Kyle's story

We encountered Kyle about a month into the project. He had lived on the streets for many years, following the break-up of his marriage and the subsequent decline in which he lost everything. Despite his own problems, Kyle offered to help in our work and, having been homeless for so long, was able to pass on some useful tips to those just starting out on the streets – safe places in which to spend the night, and so on.

Before encountering Talking Space, Kyle lacked a reason for carrying on – but today he is starting to find purpose beyond himself. While the rest of us often begrudge venturing out on rainy nights, Kyle is always first on site, despite having walked the best part of four miles to get into the city centre. He is also the only member of the team who comes along every single week. Why? Because having hit rock bottom, and then having clawed his way back, Kyle wants to help others who are facing similar issues.

Over time, Kyle has managed to get himself off the streets, and free from alcohol and drugs. Although the Talking Space team have bought him a few items for his flat (a toaster, kettle, and so on), that's about the extent of the help Kyle's allowed others to give, and he's deeply proud he's been able to achieve this all by himself. As a non-practising Muslim, it's unlikely he'll be joining us in our times of prayer any day soon – but none the less God appears to be doing something very special in Kyle's life.

Telling their stories

The homeless tend to leave us when the clubs start spilling out. First come the older clubbers at around 2am, with the younger people being turned out from the more serious dancing venues about an hour later. Some gradually make their way towards us, and each week we have a handful of deep conversations that seem to go on for hours. Hurts spill out. Fears are shared. Worries halved. 'I don't want to go home!' is a common theme, as people struggle through relationship break-ups and other crises. This isn't just the madness and mayhem of the moment, but rather the alcohol and the atmosphere often bring issues to the surface that may have been dormant for years.

Amazingly, we rarely get any trouble – because, despite the fact that Talking Space is not an explicitly Christian project, people none the less manage to make the link between the church (yard) and our work. One night a member of our team overheard one side of a mobile phone conversation that went something like this: 'Where am I? . . . Well, I guess I'm at church! . . . Yes really, church!' More seriously, one of the major issues we've faced has been among the servicemen we encounter as they return from active duty in the Middle East – many of them bearing psychological scars as a result of what they've seen and done.

Pete's story

Pete is a bomb disposal expert serving in Iraq. When we first met, his story appeared so extreme that initially we dismissed it as fiction. It was only when he started to come back to us every few months with the same developing story that we realized he was speaking the truth. He repeatedly and painfully told us about witnessing the deaths of friends and colleagues at close quarters, and seeing dead Iraqis lying in the road, in the full knowledge that his own people would have pulled the trigger. Pete told us these things not to brag, but because these images had been burnt into his soul.

Why would a rough, tough soldier want to spend his Friday nights chatting with some middle-aged people in a churchyard? The answer is because in a culture of laddishness, sometimes it's hard to be honest about our doubts, fears and insecurities. What Talking Space can offer to people like Pete is a place to be heard, where he won't be judged. It's too early to tell what will happen to Pete (I suspect he won't last much longer in the army, not after what he's experienced), but our hope is that somehow, in Christ, he will find the loving forgiveness he requires to be able to function happily once again.

Perfect? Not quite!

This is not to say that Talking Place is always the place to be on a Friday night. As a team we are each committed to covering just one night in every four weeks – as there is a heavy toll to pay the day after, which for many people is their only day off. The reality of our situation is that now, a few years into the project, we are still in constant need of new team members to replace those who drop out due to exhaustion or other commitments. Another problem we face is that this constant changeover leads to a lack of continuity from week to week, with only Kyle sticking it out every single weekend.

Looking back, I feel we made a mistake from the outset by not including 'signposts' that point to the fact that this project is about something more than providing pastoral care. We would dearly love to see a fledgling community of people who together are asking some of life's big questions – Who am I? Why am I here? Why isn't life fair? – but so far this hasn't happened. One of the most valuable lessons we have learnt is that if you don't include sufficient signposts from the very beginning, it can become increasingly difficult to move a project forward. To begin with we were so focused on losing the 'cringe factor', in sidestepping people's prejudices towards Christianity, that we developed a project that in some ways has lost its reason for being. Words without actions may well be a waste of breath, but actions without words can be equally meaningless.

I tend to describe Talking Space as being, at best, a kind of hospital – a place where those who are struggling with all kinds of life-issues can find love, support and affirmation. It provides a powerful example of Christ's care for his world. However, as an experiment in pioneering a new kind of church, it hasn't yet developed in the way we originally hoped. I've spent a lot of time thinking about this, and come to the conclusion that, if I were to engage in launching another project aimed at taking church to clubbers, I would draw from the wisdom of Vincent Donovan, a Roman Catholic missionary who attempted to build a new kind of church among the Masai in east Africa.

Christianity rediscovered

In 1965, Vincent Donovan travelled to Tanzania to be a missionary among the Masai. For the first year he worked within the existing Catholic mission compound, attached to which were a number of schools, a small chapel and a well-equipped hospital. For Donovan, however, this traditional approach of setting up an attractional mission compound, aimed at Christianizing those who came in and then sending them back out, had failed. There were no Christian Masai in the area. Although many Masai children were sent to the compound for their education, and took on the cultural trappings of the Christian religion while they were there – every single one of them left Christianity behind when they left the school. To Donovan's way of thinking this constituted a failure of the mission, and so he proposed a new approach. He resolved to leave the mission compound and to join the Masai on their own territory. Writing to his bishop, he explained simply, 'I want to go to the Masai . . . Outside of this, I have no theory, no plan, no strategy, no gimmick – no idea of what will come. I feel rather naked. I will begin as soon as possible.'[32]

Despite the major differences between the Masai of Tanzania and the clubbers of Coventry, I believe there are some shared norms between these disparate 'tribes' – in particular, the fact that, among both, the traditional Christian community is viewed as remote and irrelevant. Those who encounter Christianity often struggle to make the links between the gospel and their everyday lives, and even those who have entered into faith struggle to live out their new-found ideals in the real world.

For too long we seem to have had a 'one more heave' approach to bringing people into our churches, holding on to the dream that if we could just find that missing formula (be it loud guitars, Taizé-style worship, Alpha courses, whatever), people would come flooding back. But I think we need to wake up from this dream – to face the reality that there is no magic formula. Perhaps we shouldn't try to take people out of their communities, culture or friendship groups, and transplant them into our own – but instead should seek to work within *their* communities. Like Donovan, we perhaps need to leave the mission compound (or the church buildings) behind, and go in search of the communities that exist just outside our walls – be they the homeless, the clubbers, or whoever.

When Donovan left the mission compound behind, he travelled out into the heart of Masailand, where he entered into the Masai villages and sought permission to speak with them about God. When the village elders agreed, he then spent the next year in regular meetings talking about issues such as creation, death, salvation, and the person of Jesus Christ. Finally, after many months, Donovan felt ready to ask who was prepared to follow Christ – and he invited those who he felt had understood the message to make an individual profession of faith, and be baptized. In response to this, the elder of the village spoke up and asked, 'Padre, why are you trying to break us up and separate us?'[33]

This was because the Masai make decisions as a community, not as individuals – where one struggles to understand, another has understanding enough to help them; where one is lazy, another has energy enough to encourage them; and where one has little faith, another has faith enough to support them. This notion was in stark contrast to Donovan's experience of faith in the West. The sad fact is that many Christians, such as myself, usually think and speak of faith within the worldview of individualism – Jesus died for 'my sins', he went to the cross 'just for me', and therefore 'my personal response' should be to pray a prayer asking for his personal forgiveness. Donovan's encounter with the Masai has caused me to question this view and its appropriateness for mission in the twenty-first century. After all, once Donovan managed to get his head around the notion of community faith, the whole Masai village collectively gave themselves to Christ and were baptized together in one of the life-giving streams near their highland home – and, over time, similar baptisms occurred in villages throughout Masailand.

The idea of community is central to the Christian story, but over the years we seem to have sold out this ideal in favour of the individualism of our Western culture – so perhaps it's time we put community back at the heart of our approach to mission. Donovan's exact approach may not work with our clubbing friends, but there are many lessons we can learn from his experiences. As we journey out in search of the communities that exist beyond our church walls, perhaps we need to truly join in with them, offering our love and allowing them to love us back. Mission needs to become a two-way process, the sharing of stories, with the God-story woven into our own. We need to go to people, walk with them, and be willing to learn from them – it would be incredibly powerful if our work among clubbers produced a dialogue between our own understanding of Christianity and the value base of those with whom we are working. Together we can share a new journey, without prescribing the outcome, trusting as we go that God will be our guide. Together we can see a new kind of church emerge, one that is embedded within existing community life, by helping people to ask together some of life's big questions. As outsiders it is not our role to decide how this church will function; our job may be simply to help people encounter their creator within their own context – from there it's up to them.

A new methodology

Talking Space is still going strong, although we have currently taken a short time-out to recover our strength and reconsider the way forward. Even as I write, we are preparing for a re-launch with a team of fresh recruits, eager for the journey ahead; and as we start out once again, I have found that Vincent Donovan's experiences among the Masai have helped me to consider a new methodology for projects such as this. I have sketched this out below.

First, we need to go to people and join in with their community, or create a space where community can happen – not attempting to drag people away from their existing groups, but instead journeying together to a new place where we may encounter Christ. We need to offer our love and support within those communities, and to listen out for prayer opportunities (perhaps writing down prayer requests, and remembering to ask how things went afterwards). Through all of this, we need to be continually and prayerfully asking, 'Lord, what are you doing here?'

We need to make use of signposts as conversation starters. A signpost is something that points the way, and we would dearly wish to point the way to Christ. I'm not talking about tracts or suchlike, but something that would genuinely help those who use Talking Space to make the connection between our love and the love of Christ. This could be as simple as providing food in order to give us the opportunity to say grace together, or offering candles to be lit in remembrance of loved ones or those in need.

We need to raise questions in people's minds, and earn the right to tell our stories. When we do, we need to include our own doubts and insecurities, and avoid being prescriptive of how we expect people to respond to the gospel. Our job is to help people encounter Christ, not decide what they do next. Finally (and this is a biggie!), we need to expect to learn as much about God from those we encounter as they learn from us.

Talking Space is an ongoing project, and our thinking, learning and dreaming continue to develop. However, one thing I am convinced of is that if the Christian church in the UK is to survive this century, we need to learn the lessons from projects such as this one. If people aren't choosing to enter our church buildings, we have to accept it's because we've allowed them to become irrelevant. The task of the twenty-first-century church is surely to take the church back to the people – where it belongs.

13

Church for the Night

JON OLIVER (BOURNEMOUTH)

A little while back, some friends and I got talking about the big old traditional churches dotted around town, and about how there is often a special 'something' about these places. Of course, we all know that God is everywhere and that the church is the people and not the building, but nevertheless I really feel there can be something special about these sorts of places. Perhaps it's the fact it's consecrated ground (whatever that means) or that here the prayers of the saints have been lifted up for generations. But whatever it is, there is often such a distinct and tangible difference about these old churches that sometimes just entering these spaces, simply being there, can be a spiritual experience in itself.

We started thinking about St Peter's, a big old Gothic-style church slap bang in the middle of Bournemouth town centre – surrounded by clubs and late-night bars, one on either side of it and one right opposite. Then we started thinking about what might happen if we opened this church up overnight sometime, when all the clubs were at their busiest. Then we started thinking that probably nothing would happen, that no one would want to come in, but that we should give it a shot anyway.

So, after persuading the rector to let us have the place for the night, a bunch of us spent a month or so working out how to turn this old church from the sombre, empty, imposing building it usually seems to be at night into a magical wonderland of thought and love, contemplation and creativity. In the end, we planned music and lights and visuals and banks of TVs and projectors and sculpture and poetry and candles and prayers and (perhaps most importantly) free mince pies and mulled wine. And then, the weekend before Christmas, we opened the doors.

The night

Before we'd even opened up properly, people started coming in to have a look around, to see what was going on. They wandered about and seemed really interested in what was happening, and many promised to come back later (although, to be honest, we didn't think they would). When we went outside to set up the speaker system, we found a group of teenage girls sitting on the steps at the front. One of them was crying, and asked, 'Are you a Christian? Is the church open? Can I come in? Will you pray with me?' and before we could answer, was running through the doors. A member of the team sat and prayed with her, while the rest of us carried on setting up. With hindsight, I find it hard to believe that we didn't see the signs of what was to come, but I think we were so utterly convinced the whole evening was going to be a failure that we didn't even begin to pick up on the clues.

At 11pm we opened the doors properly, and from then on (until we finally shut them again some time after 4am) we had a constant stream of people coming in. We barely had a moment to take stock and realize how amazing it was that people wanted to come into the church, because there were so many people that we were just too busy meeting and greeting, talking about Jesus, and praying with them. Suddenly it was 3am and we were supposed to finish, but there were still people coming in, wanting to know why the church was open in the middle of the night, wanting to talk about God and to pray and to spend time in contemplation. We're talking about hundreds of people here – students, clubbers, police officers, bouncers, bar-staff, foreign students, homeless people, anyone and everyone. It was unbelievable!

The incredible thing was the fact we had no advertising – no fancy posters or flyers, no announcements in the press – and we didn't even have a proper sign outside to say what was going on. All we had were a couple of loudspeakers, a few people milling about, and a hand-written sign saying simply 'Church for the night'. During the evening I stood outside and watched for a while, and saw countless people walk by, spot the sign, and then come in without hesitation – as if this was what they had been looking for all along.

Once inside, the really unexpected thing was that people kept coming up and asking us to tell them about God. No build-up. No foreplay. Just simply, 'So tell me about Jesus.' The first time this happened, I was caught completely off guard – this flew in the face of everything I'd ever been taught about evangelism! I hadn't built up a relationship; I hadn't specifically demonstrated the love of Christ to this person; I hadn't tried to subtly introduce the topic of God into the conversation. And yet here I was, face-to-face with a complete stranger wanting to know more about Jesus. I guess this is what St Peter meant when he said we should always be ready to give an explanation for the hope we have (1 Peter 3.15). Fortunately, I recovered myself enough to be able to engage with him and find a way to relate the gospel story to his own story – and I was more pre-pared (although almost as surprised) when the next person asked me to tell them about God.

I don't want to underestimate the value of more relational forms of mission (which remain a large portion of what my life and work is all about), but it seemed that there was something about this place, something about us simply being there for these people in the middle of the night, something that God was doing in all of us, that made people want to know more right there and then. Naturally this wasn't everyone – many people came in simply out of curiosity, had a look around, and then left. Others liked what they found and stayed for a while, often just sitting quietly in their ones and their twos, sometimes lighting a candle, sometimes writing a prayer and pegging it up.

But it wasn't all just sitting on our laurels, watching people pray and waiting for them to ask us about our faith – we spent a lot of the evening wandering around, praying, checking everything was running smoothly, and making sure people felt welcome, especially as they took their first tentative steps into the building. Understandably, many people felt somewhat uncertain as they came in. (Is this really a church? Why is it open in the middle of the night? Am I allowed in? Are there any special rules for behaviour?) After all, these are people who might never have been into a church other than for the occasional wedding – in their best suits and on their best behaviour – so they didn't have any idea what to expect. We had big hand-scrawled signs telling people to make themselves at home and help themselves to mince pies and mulled wine, then we had people stationed at the church gates, some hanging around at the front door, and others waiting inside – all to welcome and guide people in, to make them feel comfortable and relaxed in what was, for many, such an alien setting. We took care to strike a careful balance between allowing people the space they needed to slow down, take stock and meet with God, while making sure we approached them with the offer of prayer or conversation at the right moments.

As the night wore on, I noticed that many people who'd said earlier they'd return did indeed come back – often with a group of friends in tow. Again, some of them came just to look at the church, but others came to stay awhile – some praying for seemingly hours at the front by themselves; others staying for a chat over mince pies and mulled wine. At one point, I serenaded a couple of lads from Zimbabwe with a song in their native tongue (which I somehow managed to remember from nearly a decade before, when I spent a few months in Africa), which paved the way for a fantastic conversation, and led to an invitation to a home-cooked Zimbabwean feast. Other members of the team found equally unexpected ways to engage with people, although it often didn't take much as the atmosphere in the church was so alive with the sense of people wanting to know more.

The church

To a certain extent the vibe wasn't all that different from some sort of alternative worship service – making interesting use of a traditional space, allowing the content and context to interact, putting together a range of different 'stations' or 'installations', and inviting people to explore at their own pace. The first thing we did was to adapt the shape of the church interior by subtly closing off certain areas, and then, by turning off the main overhead lights and positioning small pockets of light (in particular, two sets of rope-lights strung underneath the heating vents running the length of the central aisle), and having various stations at carefully spaced intervals, we hoped to draw the eye, and the visitor, down through the building to the prayer space at the front.

As for the stations themselves, we had a poetry area with poems printed up on 6-foot-high boards (some from established authors, some from our own team, some adapted from scripture); we had a contemporary sculpture of the nativity scene, which people could move in and around; and in one corner of the church there was an old, dark wooden crucifix attached to the wall, around which we assembled some rusty scaffolding that we found in the basement. Among this we set up a whole bunch of TVs playing various loops from Mel Gibson's *The Passion* (the brutality of which worked especially well in such close proximity to the warmth of the nativity sculpture), interspersed with snippets of scripture. We also had projectors throwing short films and still images on to various surfaces around the building. Finally, and probably most crucially, we borrowed the church's votive candle stand and attached a simple sign inviting people to say a prayer and light a candle.

The King's Arms

I'd like to sit
On a bar stool in heaven
Right next to Christ

We'd share a jug of beer
And a packet of smokes
(Although I doubt he'd inhale)

I think I'd tell him
About fast cars on open roads
8th birthday parties
And Arsenal's disappointing away form
I hope he'd tell me
About his favourite star
Why sheep exist
And how he thought of photosynthesis

By the second jug
We'd move to sit by the fire
Have a couple of cigars
And a packet of peanuts

I think I'd get angry
And ask him
About rape and HIV and Hiroshima and cot-death
Then he'd get even angrier
And ask me
About rape and HIV and Hiroshima and cot-death

And then
Then maybe we'd sit quietly
And sup our pints
The fire would burn
The logs would crackle
And the world would turn

After a while I'd tell him a story
He'd tell me a joke
And we'd play a few games of dominoes[34]

I think one of our biggest surprises was that despite all the thought and effort we'd put into creating the other stations, it was the simple act of lighting a candle in prayer that most caught the imagination of those who came in. This was also one of the most exciting aspects of the night – the fact that so many responded to the invitation to offer up prayers, and the opportunity to have one or more of us pray with them. There were also pens and paper to hand, and the prayers people wrote and pegged up on the prayer wall were at times both gobsmacking and heartwrenching.

At one point a group of foreign students got chatting to a member of the team, and one of them asked where he could go for confession. She explained we didn't have a confession booth but that, if he wanted, he could confess his sins directly to God – possibly even writing them on a piece of paper which could then be thrown away. He was astounded by the simplicity of it all, so she took the chance to explain to him about grace and forgiveness, and the opportunity to have a personal relationship with Jesus. At first she was worried that she would come across as preaching at him, but both he and his whole group of friends were riveted – for nearly an hour they sat on the floor around her, firing questions and listening with rapt attention to the answers she gave.

Meanwhile, we also had people organizing the music and refreshments. A couple of the team were DJs and, having set up a huge sound-system during the day, they provided us with music all night – alternating between loud thumping dance music to catch the attention of people outside, and quiet ambient tunes to help create a reflective atmosphere inside. The coffee bar was one of my favourite places in which to hang out, not only for ease of access to the mince pies, but also because this was one of the best places in which to meet people and engage in conversation – largely because it's always easier for people to open up when you're sharing a few mugs of mulled wine. Near the end of the night I was deep in conversation with one lad at the coffee bar when he was dragged away by his friends who wanted to carry on partying elsewhere. About ten minutes later he reappeared alone, telling us he'd managed to slip away from his friends when they weren't looking. We carried on the conversation where we'd left off, and he stayed for ages, even to help us pack up when we eventually closed the doors sometime after 4am.

Then at about 5.30am, when we were still cleaning up, another chap turned up wanting to pray. At first (with thoughts of my nice warm bed waiting for me at home) I apologized and told him we were closed. Then suddenly I realized I was forgetting the whole point – to be the church to people at the time when they need it, not just when it suits us. So I let him in, sat and chatted for a while, then left him to pray by himself while we packed up around him. It seemed as if the evening just didn't want to stop.

The aftermath

I had been so convinced that the whole thing was going to be a dismal failure that I hadn't even thought about the possibility of it having a future. We knew God wanted us to open the church up for this night (although to a certain extent I had thought of it simply as a test of faith), but none of us had expected that so many people would come in, let alone that we would spend the whole night talking about Jesus – at *others'* instigation! I think this was possibly the first time that I truly understood St Paul's suggestion that God can do immeasurably more than we can ever ask or imagine (Ephesians 3.20). I had imagined we would see about four people coming in, and I had hoped for maybe 40 – but God did indeed do immeasurably more than this, bringing in too many people for us to even begin to count them.

For me, one of the main outcomes of the evening was that I had to fundamentally rethink my understanding of people and their attitudes towards church. This is supposed to be a generation that doesn't give a monkey's about the church, and yet here they were, turning up in their droves – to pray, to think about God, and to talk to a bunch of Christians about the meaning of life. Naturally there were many who didn't take the opportunity to come into the church (although I saw many others who clearly wanted to, and were dissuaded by their friends), but almost everyone who did come in wanted to know when we'd be doing it again. It seemed as if everyone in town loved the idea. Some couldn't believe they were in a church instead of a club, especially as many hadn't been in a church for years (if ever), and almost none could believe they'd ended up praying with friends and strangers alike on a Friday night. At one point in the evening I saw a large group of lads charge up to the front door, looking as if they were coming in to tear the place apart – but as soon as they stepped through the front door they fell silent, and I even saw one or two of them take off their caps in quiet reverence. Although they didn't stay long, they were clearly affected by the experience. We later heard that the police were telling people about us and suggesting they should have a look, and we even saw bouncers telling clubbers as they left to come and see us, to experience 'Church for the night'. (A plentiful supply of mince pies for the bouncers might have been a contributing factor to this particular display of goodwill!)

A couple of months later, I was at a meeting with a number of local councillors and the town-centre manager (the man responsible for promoting the town's nightlife) and they too said it was a wonderful idea – mentioning that an increasing number of people are showing an interest in spirituality, and that it is through ideas such as this that they can more readily engage in exploring it for themselves. Somehow this idea has caught the imagination of people from all over, both inside and outside the church, including many who had not shown much of an interest in our work before.

'When are you doing this again? We need this again.'
'Absolutely awesome – we need night church all night every night. And I mean that!'
'Are you here every night? Church should be open like this all the time!'

Although the night was originally conceived as a one-off, with such a huge turnout and comments such as those above, we immediately realized we would have to do it again – and soon. However, we didn't want it to become an 'event' or just a 'thing we do', something to be done by rote or out of duty; we felt that if it became a weekly or monthly fixture, people would soon get bored with it (especially as it seemed that a large part of its dynamism stemmed from the unexpectedness of finding this big old church open and so full of life in the middle of the night). Instead, wanting to maintain this dynamism, we decided to wait on the Holy Spirit to prompt us when it was the right time to start planning another night. On a few occasions this has led to some frustratingly long delays, during which we have inevitably cried out to do it again sooner, but I remain convinced that this was the right thing to do – in part because we have the assurance that we are working within God's plan and not our own timetable, but also because it has meant that every single time we have come to it with a freshness and excitement that could have been lost if it had been allowed to become just another event in our busy schedules.

We have now had quite a few 'overnighters'. Sometimes we've had a theme ('true love' for Valentine's Day, or 'new life' in spring), but the recipe has basically stayed the same – more poetry, more sculpture, more art, more visuals, more fun with drinks and nibbles, and a number of increasingly innovative invitations to prayer – though always with a twist, always with something new to capture the imagination. One of my favourites was the night we covered the back of the church with grass to create a picnic area. After laying down a couple of huge tarpaulins in front of the coffee bar, we carted in around 30 square yards of turf from the local garden centre and topped it off with rugs, picnic tables, a few plants, and a waterfall projected on to one of the huge church pillars, which appeared to cascade down into the middle of it all. Add to this a few people serving cloudy lemonade and ginger ale (plus chocolate fingers, party rings, and all manner of other classic treats) and the transformation was complete – we could all enjoy a restful picnic in a summer meadow, under cover slap bang in the middle of a sprawling urban conurbation. Not quite Psalm 23, but not a bad effort.

Of course, none of this would have been possible without the tireless efforts of the team and the generous support of everyone at the church. We have been blessed with a team comprising a wealth of creativity (artists of all kinds – a painter, a sculptor, a blacksmith, and a glut of DJs and film-makers); plus a number of prayer warriors willing to spend all evening in prayer, either on their own or with the people who come in. Many others turned up simply with a heart to serve (one of whom has willingly spent hours washing the stench of urine off the steps at the side of the church, normally used by passing clubbers as the local public toilets). Had we been a different group of people, the whole place may have looked different, but as long as the three core elements – the location of the church, the prayers of the saints, and the presence of the Spirit – were in place, I'm sure the outcome would have been pretty much the same. On top of this, for a church that looks so traditional and outdated from the outside, the rector and congregation of St Peter's have been remarkably supportive of this idea from the outset, and willing to let us have free rein in their building on so many occasions – getting more excited about the good we could do than worrying about the mess we might make.

Naturally, it hasn't all been fun and games – each time it takes weeks of planning and preparation, and a whole day setting up the church before we open the doors. But it's been worth it. Every time we've seen another multitude of people finding space to stop, rest, take stock, and consider God and themselves and how the two may be able to fit together; another night filled with prayers, tears, laughter and hope; and another opportunity to demonstrate our love for God and God's love for humanity, through the outworking of the creative gifts he has given us.

We've found one of the most important things to remember is that the whole process – from the first planning meeting, through all the organization, to setting up and packing down on the night – can and should be an act of worship in itself, and absolutely has to be steeped in prayer. It's no good presenting a happy façade of loving teamwork and heartfelt kindness on the night, if we spend the preceding weeks getting stroppy with one another and allowing ourselves to become too busy to spend time with God.

Of course, we have made mistakes along the way. By our third outing we had become slightly blasé in our approach – as if it was by our own efforts that we had made this whole thing into the success it had become; as if it was through our own ingenuity and creativity that we had led people to meeting with God. We relied on our own strength, and we felt the difference. Fortunately, God didn't allow our failings to spoil his plans for the people coming in that night, but we had ignored our golden rule and had very nearly made 'Church for the night' into merely an event. This was particularly evident in our efforts to try to force a theme or a message. I once read something about the idea of worship leaders becoming like curators of an art exhibition – curators who think about space and environment as well as content; who consider the interaction between different installations, and between what is being viewed and who is doing the viewing; and who consider space and distance, colour and texture, light and shade, atmosphere and ambience, and all manner of other such things.[35] In this way, as we prepare the evening, our task is no longer to produce a mechanical procedure to deliver a predetermined message, but instead to design a context in which people can experience, participate in, and meet with God. I have toyed with this concept for years – the idea of not forcing an interpretation upon people, but allowing them to come to their own conclusions – and although this may not be an idea that we are all entirely comfortable with, it hopefully challenges us to reconsider how we go about our work. For it seems to me that conclusions we come to on our own are far more likely to stick with us than ready-made answers that are spoon-fed to us. It's about letting go, not relying on our own strength, but instead trusting in the power of the Holy Spirit to touch people's hearts and inform their decisions – just as we trust him to prompt us to prepare for another adventure in St Peter's church, just as we trust him to give us the words to speak, just as we trust him to guide our plans for the future.

And so this leaves us tottering on a terrifyingly vague but excitingly promising precipice. What does the future hold? Was this just for a season, or should we carry on for ever? If it's untenable on this scale too often, should we try something on a low-key basis more regularly, and keep the 'big' nights for special occasions? Is this idea just for us here in Bournemouth, or for elsewhere too? I don't know the answers to these questions. All I know is that when we opened a church in the middle of the night, hundreds of people showed up; when we responded to God's unpredictable call, he showed up. And I really don't think that I have ever experienced the presence of God as tangibly as I have done on these nights – when you're there for long enough, it almost feels as if you can physically touch it. I have no doubt that it's for this very reason we have seen so many people respond to him, so many offer up prayers to him, so many spend their Friday nights chatting with us in a church instead of chatting people up in a club. I remember way back on our very first night, one lad sidled up to a member of the team and whispered, 'I thought I was an atheist, but I feel God!' When God shows up in power anything can happen – our task is simply to draw people to a place where they can experience God for themselves.

14

More Beatboxing, Vicar?

GAVIN TYTE (ONLINE)

I'm a human beatboxer and an Anglican priest. Some people think this sounds like a crazy combination and a clash of stereotypes, but to me it is the most natural thing in the world. This is the story of the beginning of that journey.

A noise in church

In the early 70s, my dad bought a reel-to-reel tape recorder. Other dads were holding out for the more convenient and compact cassette players; however, this stroke of purchasing genius changed the course of my life for ever. As soon as I was old enough to play with the machine, I would plug in the microphone and make all manner of noises and drum sounds with my mouth. I would record myself and just about anything or anyone else, including the family dog. I could play back the recordings at different speeds, alternating between turning myself into a chipmunk or a monster. I still have a recording of vocal drum sounds I made in 1979 when I was just eight years old.

My parents brought me up to have a faith in God. They used to pray with me before I went to sleep each night, and up to the age of six we attended a warm, friendly United Reformed church in Doncaster. I grew up believing in God. However, when we moved south, we started attending the local Anglican church. My memories of this church are not great – it may have been fantastic, but to me it seemed old, cold and boring. The front row was full of old ladies in furry hats, and the vicar, adorned in flowing robes, would stand in the pulpit and bore into me with his eyes. What did church have to do with God?

I have to admit I wasn't exactly a golden child, and at about the same time I was recording silly noises on the tape machine, I was also making silly noises in Sunday school. After a couple of years, I stopped going altogether. My mum likes to say that I was politely asked to leave, but we both know that I was kicked out for being difficult. Nearly 30 years later, not much has changed. I still make silly noises and I am still being a challenge to the Church of England – although now I get paid to do both.

A split personality

At thirteen, I got my first hip-hop mix tape and was hooked. I loved the electronic sounds, the drum patterns and the rapping. That same year, I heard my first human beatboxing and thought to myself, 'Hey, I can do that!' And so I became a human beatboxer – someone who makes drum, DJ and instrumental sounds using just the mouth. I also began to embrace hip-hop culture, a culture that is all about self-expression through the different elements – breakdancing, graffiti, DJing, MCing and beatboxing.

By the time I was fifteen, church had stopped being about Sundays and became something that the family did at Easter and Christmas. However, my girlfriend at the time was a Christian, and one Sunday we attended her church. During the service, one of the leaders got up and gave a word of prophecy – something so specific that it could only have been God speaking to me. As you can imagine, I was quite freaked out by this. God was on my case.

Soon after this, my mum decided it would be a good idea for me to be confirmed – at least I would get to drink the communion wine at Easter and Christmas! I mentioned this to my RE teacher and he suggested I came along to his church. This church was like no church I had been to before. For a start, there were young people there. They also had drums. However, the most extraordinary thing about this church was that when the people talked to God, he seemed to be talking back!

I started going to this church, but my love of hip-hop and my love of God were kept separate. I had never heard any hip-hop or electronically produced music in church. In my life there were two cultures – church culture and hip-hop culture. Church was something that took place on Sunday, and hip-hop culture filled my world from Monday to Saturday. It never occurred to me that it could, or should, be any different.

Ordination

I regularly went to church for a couple of years and, at eighteen, after a whole heap of mind-blowing experiences of God, I gave my life to Christ. I began a career in music production, then became a designer, and finally ended up teaching music production in a college of further education.

As I grew in my faith, the gap between church culture (even contemporary church culture) and urban youth culture became more and more apparent. However, it also became clear to me that many unchurched young people were asking the same questions as I was about life, God and the universe. I often asked my students if they believed in God. Most would say, 'Yeah, I believe in some kind of God.' I would ask them what they thought of Jesus, and they would say, 'Yeah, I could be down with Jesus.' When I asked them about church, though, they would laugh and say, 'Yeah, right!' As far as they were concerned, church had nothing to do with God or Jesus – surely there was something wrong with this picture?

Human beatboxing was big in the early 80s, but by the 90s it was almost non-existent. Then, in 2000, a beatboxer called Rahzel released *Make the Music 2000*, a landmark album that featured stunning beatboxing. Some of my students played me the album and told me about this 'thing' called beatboxing. I said, 'I can do that', and they said, 'Yeah, right.' So I showed them. Lunch-hour beatboxing lessons began the next day!

A few months later, I checked out human beatboxing on the internet. There was very little available and the domain name beatboxing.co.uk was free. Two days later I went to register the domain, only to discover that someone called Alex Tew had already registered it and had put up a forum. I registered as member number three. My life as TyTe the beatboxer had begun. (By happy coincidence, my surname 'Tyte' means 'cool' in hip-hop lingo. Did God plan this or what?)

Around this time, my wife Lucy and I went on a quiet retreat to see what God might be saying to us, and returned feeling that perhaps God was calling us into the church full time. The last thing I wanted was to be a vicar but, doing our best to be obedient to God, we went to see the curate and he said, 'Yes, you had better go and see the vicar.' We went to see the vicar and he said, 'Yes, you had better go and see the diocesan director of ordinands.' So we went to see the diocesan director of ordinands and she said, 'Yes, you had better go and see the bishop.' Nine months, 23 meetings, and a lot of prayer later, I was accepted to train for ordination in the Church of England.

I spent a final year teaching, and during this time I contributed to the new online beatboxing community (which had now changed its name to humanbeatbox.com) through articles, reviews and free beatboxing tutorials. The site began to grow, and later that year I found myself doing beatboxing gigs in universities and clubs, including the finals of the German DJ championships.

World beatboxing community

Theological college was not an easy ride. I liked the theology, the college community, and made some lifelong friends, but the training was for parish ministry (to be a vicar or parish priest) and in my heart, I didn't want to be a vicar. But, despite feeling like a round peg in a square hole, there were some glimmers of hope. First, there was the idea of 'sector' ministry – I felt much more affinity with those working in industry as chaplains than with those who wanted to be parish priests (although I was saddened to discover nearly all the sector ministers I came across held a theology that meant they barely wanted to tell anyone about Jesus – it was more presence than proclamation). Second, there was a rising tide of people promoting emerging church or fresh expressions of church. When I heard Graham Cray speak about church connecting with culture, it was as if the penny had dropped. Now I knew why I was doing this!

What's in a name?

In hip-hop culture, people have a street name. My street name is TyTe (the use of capitals is important – don't ask me why, it just is). This idea of having a pseudonym has been carried over into web forums. I suppose, for a hip-hop-related site, it makes lots of sense. Some people think that using a street name is about hiding behind a cover, or somehow veiling our true identity. To us, it is the most natural thing in the world to be called by our street name. I know Jason's real name. It's erm, Jason! However, whenever I chat to him online or see him in person I call him Yas (short for yasSon, his street name). The thing is, on a web forum, it's pretty much like real life. People let you see as much of them as they want to. It takes time to make friends and, at the end of the day, people are people whether they have a street name or not. It's just a name.

While studying at Trinity College in Bristol, I connected with the local hip-hop scene and held some beatboxing jams at Hope Chapel. I put the word out on humanbeatbox.com and people travelled from all over to come and beatbox. Around this time, through connecting with Christians who were into hip-hop, one of the young beatboxers came to know Jesus. Clearly, God was using beatboxing to reach people. There was church culture and hip-hop culture, and somehow the two were coming together.

Meanwhile, on humanbeatbox.com, another ministry was developing. Alex Tew (aka A-Plus) ran the site for the first three years. He wanted to make the site commercially successful, but after three years it had not developed as he'd hoped – though the community forums had really taken off, with membership having grown to over 6,000. By now I was doing a lot of Christian ministry with members on the site. Some of the longest discussions on the forums were about spirituality, and I found myself in the position of counselling and praying for young beatboxers about a range of problems.

How does a community forum work?

A forum is a way of communicating through a website. You post messages in a forum. People can post replies to the initial message and, together with the initial message, these are called a thread. So a forum usually consists of many threads. The thread with the most recent message or reply stays on the top. Oh, it is too difficult to explain – go to humanbeatbox.com, click on the FORUM link and take a look for yourself! Have you done it? Cool. I believe you! Right. So one of the most common questions is, 'What's to stop someone posting something abusive?' The answer is, 'Nothing.' You cannot stop someone posting an abusive message or reply. In fact, it happens all the time. Sometimes a discussion gets heated and a member lets rip at another member. Sometimes someone posts spam (unsolicited messages) advertising sex, pornography, Viagra, or some other dodgy products. Sometimes you just get creepy people posting creepy messages. The good news is that we have a team of what we call moderators. These are people whose job it is to read every post on every thread and edit or delete inappropriate messages. They also have the power to ban members. On the whole, this works very well – as long as you have plenty of good moderators. In fact, I would go so far as to say that good moderation is key to the success of a community forum. They have to be sensitive, diplomatic and very dedicated.

Trendy vicar syndrome

In 2004, as a continuation of my training, I took up a post as a curate (assistant vicar) just outside Southampton. A few months later, Alex decided to sell humanbeatbox.com. I prayed as to whether to buy the site, but could only offer Alex a small amount of money. He kindly accepted my offer, mainly because he felt I was the best person to run the site, and so I became the owner and manager of humanbeatbox.com. (Alex went on to develop the phenomenally successful website www.milliondollarhomepage.com!)

Word about me being a beatboxing priest got around. In an interview with the BBC, the news presenter proposed that I was living proof that the Church of England was trying to be trendy. I think the exact phrase was 'vicars in leather jackets'. I'm not sure 'trendy' is a word I associate with the Church of England, although I would describe it as 'cutting edge'. This may surprise you, because popular opinion suggests that the Church of England is out of date and out of touch – but history shows that it's also out of bounds! The Anglican Church has been one of the most innovative and creative forces in the UK for, well, as long as the Church of England has existed – and with hardly a leather jacket in sight!

Not just a forum

The humanbeatbox.com community is not just focused around the website. Many of the community communicate online using email, instant messaging, networking websites or via speech communication programmes. Then there are regional gatherings called jams, where groups of beatboxers gather together to jam *a cappella*, usually in a park or public place. There are also more formal gatherings such as gigs, championships or conventions. In fact, meeting face to face is much more common than you might think – even though it does involve a lot of travel. It's great fun meeting for the first time someone you have chatted to online for years.

Developing theology

Over the past few years my theology (that is, my understanding of the nature and purpose of God) has changed and developed, and is still changing and developing. I have been profoundly challenged by authors such as Tom Wright, Brian McLaren, Dallas Willard and Rob Bell, who have all helped shape my thinking. One of the things they all have in common is the way they are prepared to examine and re-examine the church and their own ministry in the light of Jesus' ministry. I love this openness, honesty and commitment to being true to their first love, and I consistently try to do the same. As I have grown in my understanding, I have come to recognize that my initial passion to bless and transform the beatboxing community with the love of Jesus is theologically sound; Christians are called to be salt and light in the world, to build the kingdom of God, and to see lives transformed with the love of Jesus.

A few months into my first post as a curate, I told the bishop what I was doing in the beatboxing community, and all about the exciting things happening. He decided to release me from my parish duties one day a week to continue the beatboxing ministry. (See what I mean about the Church of England being cutting edge?) So this is exactly what I did.

Doing evangelism online

I think over the past six years I have tried just about everything in terms of evangelism. I've tried apologetics, I've had email conversations that went back and forth for months, I've tried prophetic evangelism, pathetic evangelism, you name it! So what works? That's the million-dollar question. What works? Well, first, prayer works. It's amazing how many times things seem to shift in the attitudes of people when I pray – and yet I still find prayer the most difficult thing. Prayer in every form works: silent prayer when typing, prayer for people just before you go to bed, emailing prayers to people, or offering to pray as you chat online. Prayer works. Second, being yourself works.

Blasting people with a hell-fire gospel message that 'Jesus saves and you need to believe now!' does not work. It just puts people off, or adds fuel to the idea that Christians are closed-minded. Loving works. Serving works. Not letting angry words spill out on the page works. Not retaliating when people hurt you works. Being willing to help a newbie works. Listening works. Being open and honest about your failures as well as your successes works. I once did an interview for a secular music magazine and one of the questions was, 'TyTe, you are respected in the beat-boxing community. How do remain so grounded?' Now there was an opportunity . . . !

So how do we do church online?

In the three years after I took over, the humanbeatbox.com membership grew from around 6,000 members to well over 40,000, and it is still growing phenomenally. Notably, within that time, 'I' has become 'we'. A small crew of beatboxers who are also Christians continue to seek to bless the beatboxing community, giving our time and skill to this community because we love beatboxing. We also engage in evangelism and pastoral care, and we have seen young people deal with various personal problems, including one who decided against suicide as a result of the support of the online beat-boxing community. It doesn't get much more real than that! We have seen people come to know Jesus through the relationships made on the site, and several members of the community have been baptized in their local churches.

The secret of success

What did I do to grow a website from 6,000 members to over 40,000 in three years – bearing in mind that you don't actually have to be a member to access the site? Well, I hate to admit it, but I stuck to a very basic principle that I learned from Bill Gates. I have been in the web business for about 15 years, and one of the first things I ever learnt was his declaration that

'Content is King'. Well, Bill was wrong, Jesus is King, but he's got a point! By focusing on creating great content for humanbeatbox.com (such as free audio and video tutorials, reviews, interviews and competitions) I built the site into the best resource on the web for beatboxing, both in terms of quantity and quality. I used technology that enabled and encouraged the community to create content too, which helped it grow bigger and better every day. Serving a community builds community. No secret agendas, no trying to make money off the back of members – just serve because you love.

But is it church?

My answer to this question has to be yes and no. It seems to me that people today belong to different networks. Times have changed. The traditional network would have been geographically based, a parish or village or suburb, and even work-based or leisure-based networks are geographical to some extent. Now we have internet-based networks that breach geographical boundaries – and these can be just as robust as traditional networks. On humanbeatbox.com, for example, some of the members are real friends and talk daily; the relationships are very strong, yet we rarely meet face to face. So, to one extent, we are church because we are a strong community of Christians giving each other pastoral care and seeking to live in and bless the wider beatboxing community. Yet we are not church, in the sense that we cannot physically worship together, break bread together, or give each other a real, live hug when we need one. So, currently, all the Christians on humanbeatbox.com belong to more than one Christian community. There is their online church and their offline church.

This has led to another situation. One of the members who became a Christian through the beatboxing community started going to her local church, and was baptized there. After a while, though, she stopped attending because the community that she felt a real part of was humanbeatbox.com. Her culture is urban music and hip-hop. Her local church, even though it was on the lively end of things, was still part of a completely alien culture. She hasn't given up on her faith – far from it. It's just that the local church doesn't do it for her, and she feels like an outsider. We Christians sing our own hymns or soft-rock ballads and have our own way of doing things. Why should we expect a young urban artist to change her culture? There are some things that the offline church just doesn't seem able to do.

What is the answer? I don't know! We're still working on it.

Another question I keep asking myself is 'Who will fund this ministry?' In the Church of England there are currently no grants available for doing church in a non-geographical arts network. The parish will not fund it because it is non-parochial. The diocese will not fund it because it is cross-diocese. I happened to be very lucky in having a bishop who 'got it' and let me have some time to do it alongside my parochial ministry. But what about the others?

Not so fresh?

I think that the true definition of a 'fresh expression of church' is a church that is seeded out of an existing community, be it geographical or network based. Alternative worship services and church plants are good things – no, they are *great* things – but they are not necessarily fresh expressions. In some ways, humanbeatbox.com has the potential to be a true fresh expression of church. I think it actually would be if we all lived a bit closer!

The sad fact is that I often wonder whether we as a church have really grasped the idea. I see lots of deaneries and dioceses pumping money into 'fresh expressions' where someone wants to start a new kind of service – but surely this needs to be about new kinds of *being* church? I once visited a 'fresh expression' that took place in an Anglican church. It was a service for students. It was in a Vineyard style. It was great, but I wasn't entirely sure that it was a fresh expression, and wondered how it got labelled as such. In my heart of hearts, I hope deaneries and dioceses will invest in true pioneers and missionaries to the culture of our day – men and women who will grow unique, weird and wonderful species of church. What will they look like? Put simply, they will look like what they look like.

The future

In 2007, after many years of growing the community, I took the decision to sell humanbeatbox.com to one of its trusted and hard-working members. It got to the point where I was spending more time managing the site than doing ministry (by which I mean talking to people and inputting into their lives). The site was getting over 100,000 visitors per month, and it needed someone who had the time and skills to manage such a large site – or at least raise the funds to make it viable. The new owner is not a Christian, but I don't think that matters. I've done my bit for that community, and I'm still a member. Ministry won't stop because someone else owns the land – or, in this case, the server.

I don't know what the future holds. God is doing amazing things through humanbeatbox.com. All I have to do is keep my eyes fixed on Jesus.

15

God Bless Ibiza

VICKY WARD (IBIZA)

It's a cold summer's day in England. Once again the rain hasn't stopped and I can barely remember what a blue sky looks like. I sit here daydreaming of the last few summers in Ibiza, with clear blue seas, white sand, endless sunshine and cool cocktails – remembering all the fun and madness of the last few years of hot summers abroad, while attempting to find the words to tell the story (so far) of what happened when 24-7 Prayer collided with the small but significant island of Ibiza.

The White Isle

Ibiza is a small island in the Mediterranean, just off the Spanish coast, with a resident population of under 100,000, although during the peak of the summer season numbers on the island swell to well over 300,000 at any one time. Alongside sweeping white sand beaches, chilled-out bars, bronzing bodies and the hustle'n'bustle of everyday Ibicenco life, Ibiza has been marked on the map by its infamous ability to host some of the world's best clubs and throw some of the most prestigious after-parties. It has become the high place of club culture, attracting hedonist clubbers from all over the world.

On the surface Ibiza's image is glamorous: beautiful people adorn

151

the podiums of Pacha, Amnesia, Privilege and other 'must go' establishments; sophisticated sexiness oozes from those meandering their way through the small arcane bars of Ibiza's main town; and cool contented revellers happily clap and cheer as the sun sets behind the sparkling blanket of sea in front of Sunset Strip. The dream seems too good to be true, and many people fall madly in love with the island.

However – having spent countless nights picking up intoxicated individuals from the pavement, while trying not to get vomit stuck in between our flip-flops, and calling ambulances for people rendered unconscious from over-indulgence and deadly cocktails of drink and drugs – it soon becomes clear that all that glitters is not gold, and the cracks in the alluring façade begin to appear.

So how did we end up in Ibiza?

We went to Ibiza mainly because we were invited. Early in 2000 a group of us who were involved in different ways in the 24-7 Prayer movement got together and shared our 'what if' ideas of going to Ibiza to see what God was up to. Some of us were into the club scene, some weren't, but all of us were up for seeing God impact a generation of young people who hadn't yet met their Maker. Around the same time, Pete Greig, the founder of 24-7 Prayer, was approached by Sara Torres (a member of the English-speaking church in Ibiza) at the Contra-Corriente gathering in Spain, who asked if 24-7 Prayer would come to Ibiza and help the churches to pray. Through this timely merging of dreams, we found ourselves plotting, planning and preparing for a trip to this small Mediterranean island.

At that time there was a lot of talk about advancing God's kingdom in the emerging generations by making Jesus relevant and real. This meant being in the world, living kingdom values, and becoming influencers among the influencers. It was about identifying the high places in youth culture, places that set the pace and dictated the way of life by their 'who, how, where, when' trend-setting. If influential world pioneers were impacted by the gospel, surely it would send ripples of truth and revival out across other nations, generations and cultures? The gossiping of the gospel, it coming alive and relevant to communities of people who don't fit into church as we know it. The heralding of the weirdos, and the summoning of the losers and freaks. What if we dared to go like Caleb and cross into the promised land to check it out? What would we find? Who would we meet? What was God doing on the White Isle, if anything?

Our trip also came close on the heels of Ibiza's very public 'outing' – in January 1998, the outrageous escapades that make up the party scene in Ibiza (excessive drug-taking, drunken revellers, sordid sex acts within the clubs) were sensationally exposed in the *Ibiza Uncovered* documentary series. In fact, Ibiza's 'outing' was so bad that the British vice-consul resigned from his position, likening the island to a modern-day Sodom and Gomorrah. The damage was done, the reputation stuck, and with this in mind we asked ourselves, 'Does God *really* love Ibiza? Can he *really* want to hang out and befriend people in this place?' We soon decided that, seemingly contrary to popular opinion, the answer was a definite yes! As a result, a small group of us jetted off in September 2000 for a week in Ibiza – not knowing who we would meet, where we would stay, or what checking out the lie of the land would mean for us as individuals, as a group, for 24-7 Prayer, the body of Christ, the church on the island, and the island itself.

September 2000

We were met at the airport by Sara Torres and her mum, Julia, who let us have the use of a wonderful apartment on the top of their beautiful white-washed house. We were welcomed, loved, accepted and, as the hot Mediterranean sun drenched our minds and bodies with its pure rays, we talked almost unendingly about Ibiza's history and their love for the island. We hadn't known what we would find within the churches, but were encouraged to discover a number of vibrant communities that clearly loved Jesus. They were active, alive, praying, loving and accepting. They were also frustrated by the annual summer invasion, watching their home being trashed while they sat by wondering how to reach out and respond. During our long conversations, we all shared our dreams and visions, passions and longings for Ibiza. As a team we learnt a great deal about the love of the local church for Ibiza, and about how they faithfully prayed for God to lavish his blessing on the island, its people and its visitors.

One particular afternoon we met with the leaders of three key churches, and were put through our paces as they showered us with questions: 'Why did we want to come to Ibiza? What did we want to do? Were we prepared to work with the local churches, under their leadership?' We had a lot to prove, and rightly so. In understanding Ibiza, it's important to appreciate that this island has a long history of being invaded by foreigners, who exploit its riches and then move on leaving it desecrated, or are moved on by successive raiders – Phoenicians, Carthaginians, Romans, Vandals, Barbarians, Byzantines, Arabs, Catalans and the Pirates have all left their mark on the land. Today it could be suggested that the same pillaging of the island occurs through tourism, especially by us Brits! We come, we party, we consume and devour and throw away what we don't want – leaving the island and its people to deal with the aftermath. With this legacy in mind, the island's churches wanted to be sure we weren't coming to do the same – to conquer Ibiza, to be the next big thing.

That evening, as we prayed together, two important things happened. First, one of our team felt God prompt her to publicly apologize for how the British had treated the island in recent years, and to ask for forgiveness for the damage caused to the island. The Holy Spirit moved in a big way, and began a healing process among the churches, between us, and the British and Spanish communities. We realized that the only way to establish ourselves in Ibiza was to submit to what God was already doing and to learn from our new friends how to serve, bless and pray for the island. Second, the churches shared that, for 20 years, they had prayed that a group of young people, who loved Jesus and were both real and relevant in their faith, would come to Ibiza and immerse themselves in the culture to reach the younger generations. They were also brave enough to share with us some of the prophetic words they had received over the years – words that spoke of God's love for Ibiza and his redemption plan for the island, given by reliable leaders, weighed, and held to be true among the churches on the island. Here are a few snippets of these prophetic words:

For so long many have come to Spain to party and partake in the spirit of the world. But I am turning the tables and I declare the church will celebrate and the world will take notice and the partying on earth will be to a new tune and will be an echo of my angels in heaven as they celebrate salvations . . . people will come on holiday with no agenda for salvation, but instead they will have profound encounters with me.

Part of the redemptive purpose for Ibiza and Spain is to restore the worship of the living God in Europe. This is your inheritance. God is going to redeem the music culture and he has provided a whole generation for revival, because the generation is a musical generation.

Ibiza will become a place of pilgrimage for those who are looking for God and to worship. There will be a new sound from heaven inspired by the Holy Spirit, angelic worship. The world will try to copy it but won't be able to and the lovers of music of all Europe will come to listen to this sound. They will come for the music but they will find the source of the music.

God's purpose for this island is that it will be a centre for worldwide evangelism. Everyone who comes from different parts of the world to celebrate sin will find a people that are righteous in God, that are living in God; they move in the power of the resurrection of the Lord and live to serve a just God. This will make them return to their countries changed.

Some of God's ideas are ridiculous. The strategy is a group of praisers going in front of the army.

Through spending time with the local Christians, we were reminded that what we were hoping to do was not about us, but about being part of Ibiza's history and journey. Before we were born, God was moving on the island, and will continue to do so long after we have perished. With the help of these Christians, we captured something of God's heart for Ibiza, which in turn helped us realize that our being here wasn't just about having a prayer-room, reaching out to clubbers, and squeezing in some quality dancefloor time – it was about so much more! It was about a nation and a generation that wasn't confined to British clubbers; it was also about the Spanish, the Italians, the Germans – in fact, anyone who loved Ibiza and loved to party. It was about Europe. It was about the world. Suddenly our dreams felt small in comparison to God's desires for his lost people and creation.

To hear these Christians' stories, and to be told we were part of an answer to their faithful non-stop prayer for young people to come out and interact with the generation they so loved but struggled to relate to, was mind-blowing and humbling. It broke our hearts, and provided final confirmation that we were to return to Ibiza and walk with these people on the next part of the adventure. Our question was, what mark were we going to make as part of that journey, what legacy were we going to leave behind? Maybe we were the group of praisers who were to go in front of the army . . . Me? Us? *Ridiculous!*

Summer 2002

In June 2002, seven of us packed our suitcases and flew over to spend two and a half months in Ibiza. At last, it was the start of the summer we had all been waiting for. Our home was a villa on the wooded red-earthed slopes of a tiny rural village. To be honest, it wasn't the best location (being a half-hour drive from San Antonio, one of Ibiza's main tourist towns, and where our prayer-room was based), but it was cheap and it was certainly beautiful. We spent most of our time in San Antonio, hanging out, making friends, engaging in mission, and bringing something of Jesus into play. During the summer we were joined by four teams of 15 people for two weeks at a time, who joined us clubbing, serving the people we met, giving out fruit to intoxicated individuals, prayer chatting (praying as we walked through town), and gathering prayer requests from people along the way. A couple of the lads on the team were DJs, and over the summer they managed to get a regular slot in the West End (the main clubbing strip in San Antonio), from where they threw free parties for people to enjoy. They also held DJ-workshops in one of the bars on Sunset Strip – where countless clubbers chill during the day and wind up to partying at night, after watching the sun set over the glistening waters.

Our aim through all of this was to *pray, play* and *obey*.

Praying for Ibiza, for the tourists, for the seasonal-workers living there, as well as to bless and encourage the existing church communities on the island. *Playing* hard, having fun, making new friends, going out clubbing and partying, catching strong, lazy Spanish coffees, chilling on the golden beaches – enjoying and appreciating all of the island. *Obeying* God by living as followers of Jesus; watching our alcohol intake, choosing to bless and give away our goodness freely; and abstaining from the empty promises of the sex, drugs and rock'n'roll lifestyle devoured by many on the island.

At times this was really hard. The summer was full of fun and laughter, but also tears and frustrations – we lived on top of each other with little room or personal space; it even rained on every single one of our days off! However, God remained faithful and, as we took some risks, tried new ideas, and pushed ourselves to engage with our generation, stories started to emerge. We quickly learned that this summer wasn't about 'numbers' or 'converts'. In fact, although we prayed for loads of people that first summer, not one of them gave their life to Jesus. So often in Christiandom we measure success by how many people become Christians, join activities, or sign up to the next programme. For us it was about learning to find a rhythm of grace and Christ-centred love for the countless people who don't yet know him.

One story I remember is of a dancer who worked at the world-famous Eden nightclub, where some of our team went clubbing one night. While they worshipped through dance and engaged with the often-spiritual lyrics of the music being pumped out, one of the team felt God had something to say to one of the female dancers. He tentatively approached her while she was resting by the bar, and introduced himself. They got chatting, and during the conversation he told her that he was a Christian and that God wanted to let her know that God loved her. The woman stopped in her tracks as tears welled in her eyes – she explained that this was the fourth time in the past three years that a Christian had approached her to give her the same message. Although she didn't fall to her knees at that moment, it was clear that God was leading her on a journey, and through our team member taking the risk of sharing something of God's love with her, she was reminded that she wasn't alone, nor forgotten.

New life

One of the most amazing things we got involved with that first summer was cleaning some of the island's beaches. As a team, we were convinced our prayers also needed to be practical, so via our friends in the local churches we arranged to work with the government's environment agency, cleaning part of the national nature reserve (which, as it happens, was also the gay nudist beach!). On our first day we were stunned into silence when the park ranger explained the impact that tourism, and the resulting litter and pollution, had upon the island's natural habitat. The increase over the previous decades had meant that certain flower species had stopped growing, turtles had ceased laying their eggs on the beach, and other species of wildlife were being poisoned by the litter, or had disappeared from its shores altogether. It was humbling to realize our actions could so directly affect the land God has given us to tend and nurture. So, armed with rubber gloves, big rubbish bags and plenty of water, we set about cleaning the beach. This was our prayer, a practical expression that reflected our desire for God to restore the island to its original beauty, to how he had made it to be.

It wasn't glamorous work. In fact, it was the complete opposite, and we had many moments of wanting to give up. Cleaning the beach meant getting up very early to avoid the midday sun, working extremely hard, and getting very sweaty and dirty. We removed all sorts of bits from the beach – used condoms, old tyres, plastic bottles, tin cans, used syringes, an old mattress, porn magazines, carrier bags, even a washing machine . . . you name it, we cleared it. Over the weeks, we got used to explaining what we were doing to the intrigued men and women who came to enjoy lazy hours in the sunshine, and who generally wore little more than flip-flops and a rucksack. Our dusty smiles and our pidgin-Spanish 'Hellos' amused, bemused and challenged them all at the same time. A few weeks later, after we had moved to clean another stretch of the beach, a rather excited environmental ranger came to find us. Again his words silenced us: a flower species thought to be extinct had started growing again in the sandy crevices of the first beach we had cleaned. It had been spotted in several places in full delicate bloom and was beginning to re-establish itself at a vigorous rate . . . YEEESSSSSSSSSS!!!

It was the smallest, barely noticeable but most extraordinary sign that God was answering our prayers. It occurred to us that as we physically cleansed the land, God was spiritually cleansing it, and our act of removing the stinking rubbish was parallel to God removing the rubbish that can entangle our lives. We also learnt that coming to Ibiza wasn't just about pursuing our passions and visions for Jesus in club culture (and to get in some good dancing), it was about something much bigger – falling in love with a nation. It was learning that dualism doesn't exist in God's world, and that we couldn't just be there for the clubbers because, if it wasn't for the island itself, then neither they nor us would be there in the first place. We had to learn to care for this small corner of creation and to nurture it. As we did, God nurtured us too, allowing us to begin laying the foundations that would be built upon over the coming years.

The local churches

From the outset we knew our relationships with the local churches would be key in establishing a 24-7 Prayer community in Ibiza. It was amazing to be so accepted straight away, and released to bring something new and fresh to Ibiza, that also complemented what the island's Christians were already doing and included them in the process. The churches continually reminded us to look between the lines and behind the scenes – they helped us to see the different aspects of the island and how to love all of it, even the bits glossed over by the media and the tourist industry. In so many ways their wisdom, experience and insight into living and working in Ibiza, and their prayers, helped carry us through all the summers we lived on the island. They loved to pray – loudly, and for a long time – and gave us a building to use as our prayer-room. They also taught us about spiritual warfare, how to pray for Ibiza, which particular battles to fight, and how to withstand the dark nights that occasionally robbed us of peace while we were there.

Strangely enough, their church culture was very strict compared to ours. They deplored having the clubs on the island and the culture they promulgated, and would rather have seen the clubs permanently closed. They struggled to understand our passion for the clubs, let alone how we could worship in them – but despite this they chose to try and understand our culture, to invest in us, and support us every step of the way. I guess we all learnt something from each other, and recognized that our strengths and limitations complemented each other. They taught us to understand Spanish culture and embrace it while we lived there; we taught them that youth culture wasn't something to fear and that one could still live a Jesus-centred life in the midst of this.

As for the individuals who supported us, there are too many names to mention, but I'm sure we would have burned out a long time before our first summer had ended if it hadn't been for their kindness. They took us into their homes, kept us fed and refreshed, listened patiently when we found the going tough, let us crash out with films or pool-time when we were homesick, and acted as our translators when the cars got towed away because we'd parked them in the wrong places! They also let us in on the secret locations of the island's most beautiful beaches.

It was an incredible experience. We learnt so much, and realized that mission is often as much about what God does in our own lives, as how he uses us in others'. We had played a small part in God's plans for Ibiza, but eventually the summer faded and, like the tide ebbs from the shore, the tourists and summer workers returned home. We too packed our bags and headed for the airport – tired, fulfilled, glad to be going home, but anticipating if and when we would return to be included in the next step of the adventure.

Summer 2003

The following June we got back on the plane, and waited for the bumpy landing into Ibiza airport. Touchdown on Ibiza always raises a deep excitement; walking off the plane and breathing in the hot dusty air of this Mediterranean island evokes a sense of 'coming home', of finally returning to the place where our souls and spirits can truly be free. I have yet to find another place where I connect with God in the way I can in Ibiza. What is it about this island that is so alluring? Chatting to friends who don't share my faith, I found they too experience the same excitement, and plan the next Ibiza adventure within a week of returning home from the last one.

Our second summer in Ibiza saw us staying at a hostel in the centre of San Antonio, and we felt more prepared, having reflected upon last year's trials, learning curves and fun times during the intervening months. This time the teams coming out to join us were slightly smaller and more spaced out, in order to help us find a healthier rhythm of praying, playing and obeying. Between us we would pray 24-7 in the prayer-room, and go out walking, praying and chatting in the West End at night. We went dancing and worshipping in the clubs, cleaned the wastelands, gave out water to clubbers, carried semi-conscious people back to their hotels – the list could go on. Again it wasn't always easy, yet these team members dared to take risks, step out of their comfort zones, and allow God to use them in all sorts of ways. Bruce Gardiner-Crehan was one of these team members, and here he tells some of his story:

Ever since I began listening to dance music at the age of sixteen, my dream had always been to go to Ibiza, to be part of the buzz that emanated from this small island in the sun. I had heard so much about it – on TV, in dance magazines, from friends who had been – all saying how amazing it was. The music I listened to had its roots in Ibiza, having been inspired by the sounds of the island, or having been a massive 'choon' there that particular season. A number of different opportunities to go to Ibiza came up, but for various reasons my plans never materialized, and it was not until I was in my mid-twenties that I finally made it out there – although I never thought it would happen this way.

In the last year of my degree course, with little money to my name, I heard about 24-7 Prayer going on mission trips around the world, trying to be light in dark places. I couldn't think of a better way to fulfil my dream of going to Ibiza than to be a part of what God was doing on the island through some crazy clubbing Christians. And so the adventure began . . .

My very first evening in San Antonio's notorious West End ended with me having the opportunity to pray for three people. It was magical. I thought this is it, there's no place I'd like to bless more – making a difference with people in the heart of Ibiza's club scene, praying with clubbers who are desperately interested in God and in Ibiza. My parting words were for them to find out more about God by trying to get along to a local church. I went to sleep that night with a huge smile on my face.

Soon a peculiar love affair began. I was drawn into it. It's hard to describe what 'it' is. Maybe it's the best dance music, the world-famous clubs, the superstar DJs, the beautiful sunsets every night, or the people from every corner of the globe gathering to dance the night away; maybe it's the thousands of British workers flocking there each year and forming some sort of strange community over the summer months. Yet there was something much deeper. I felt privileged to be able to get to know some of these people, to serve them in simple ways, to pray for them, to help practically. For me, to partner with the churches on the island, to set up a prayer-room, to ask for God's blessing to be poured out on my generation – that was what it was about. Everything else, the clubs, the music and the reputation – that was my context.

I went out again in 2005 when the Heasleys had just arrived. The following two years I returned again, both times to co-lead a team and help develop the vision of 24-7 Ibiza. Looking back, so much had changed from the first time I was there – there now seemed such an openness from the British workers and owners of the bars / clubs, which I hadn't experienced before. Where there was fear, there is now trust. Where there was ridicule, there is now respect. I think it's because those who live and work out there during the summer now know that we're serious about making a difference; our actions speak louder than our words.

I'd never spent so long in A&E before last summer. The staff couldn't quite work us out. I sat there on many long nights, having just carried in another overdosed or alcohol-poisoned clubber. Often I would bump into one of them the following night, and they would run up to me with affection, hugs, apologies, but mainly thanks. They would say: 'You saved my life!' Yet it never felt that we were doing anything special, it felt just the most natural thing to do: picking someone up from the floor, seeing if they're OK, offering help. Sometimes I didn't get to give an answer as to why I was doing what I was doing, but that didn't matter. I thought about secretly leaving a Christian tract in their pocket, but quickly dismissed the notion. You kind of trust that God will bring something from this. Maybe I'll get to tell them why I did what I did, but maybe I won't. My hope is that I'll see them again next year . . .

The summer team worked closely with the short-term teams, backing them up, taking responsibility for their safety, and being on hand to chat and pray if the going got tough. Each of us had a specific role, although it took us a while to work out how to facilitate the teams without us all ending up doing everything at once. We were enormously grateful for the life, fun, friendship, enthusiasm and integrity that the short-term teams brought with them. Each team had its own unique characteristics that influenced what happened, but all of them helped us to reach out to, pray for, and love Ibiza, its people, workers and tourists in ways we'd never have been able to manage on our own. They challenged us to keep on when the going got tough, and taught us how to release them into their potential while cheering them on from the sidelines. They were a key factor in consolidating our presence on the island. They prayed hard, partied hard, and helped pick up even more rubbish than we had managed the previous year; they were the dynamic, faith-filled bursts of energy that made the summer, and kept us on our toes. This poem, written by a team member, and pinned up in the prayer-room, sums up the attitude and passion of those who came out on short-term teams:

In it to win it

Come on Ibiza
Blowing it up Team B
Come one come all
The bond of love will not die
Though stretched and turned, attacked and burned
We will not let each other down
Or let up on the spiritual assault
Of the high places, the strongholds
And the spiritual authorities
We are claiming victory over this summer
The family of five who broke the doors down

Bring it on
Come one, come all
Ripping it up, smashing it down
Because there is One in Heaven who wears the crown
His sovereignty is absolute
Reality will bend as His rescue plan of love is advanced
Desperately we must seek Him
Throwing off all that holds us back or pulls us down
Obsessively, dangerously, undeniably
The faith of the mustard seed is our weapon
To fight the ridiculous fight

Hedonists for Jesus turning hedonists to Jesus
Let it flow, don't hold it back or say no, to the little voice that
Calls us on deeper, harder, faster, weaker
In Him and for His glory
Let's ride this one out
Cos we are already gambling our lives on the Cross
Let's gamble each day on Him and the Spirit which transforms us
By the renewing of our minds and strengthening of our bodies
Soaring like eagles, not in pride or arrogance, arguing and fighting
But in humble service, loving those who we find on the journey
Taking advantage of every opportunity, and refusing to stop or let up
Ferocious in prayer and obedience
Love marks us, sparks us, rules us, kills us, resurrects us, is us

(Anonymous)

Summer 2004

As we began our third summer in Ibiza, the shape of our 24-7 community changed again. Once more the churches supported us, and the short-term teams came and went with as much energy, passion and perseverance as before, but this time round some members of the summer team worked in the bars and clubs, or as promoters for various club nights. Tim Hirst worked as a PR assistant-manager for one of the big-named nights on the island, and it was through him that our community first met Carlos. Here Tim tells his story:

We first met Carlos outside a tacky bar on the main West End strip, in the heart of San Antonio. He was working as a PR for the bar we were throwing some parties at and, with his fine Latino looks and cheeky smile, he had a distinct knack for getting the ladies in. Over the summer we became firm friends with Carlos, regularly hanging out and going clubbing together. One day he told us that he had some questions he wanted to ask about our faith, and asked if we could meet up.

After numerous stand-ups, we eventually met up right at the end of the summer. Carlos asked us all sorts of questions about Jesus, which we tried to answer as best we could, but then something clicked – the Holy Spirit was powerfully present, and each of us had things we thought God had told us to say to Carlos. We knew a small amount about his life already (that he'd entered Spain illegally, that without official papers he couldn't get a secure job, and that he was living in a squat), but the things we felt God wanted to say to Carlos were related to stuff that had happened in his distant past, that we should have known nothing about – so it was either incredible guess-work or God speaking through us! Moved by what he was hearing, Carlos asked if we would pray for him. We agreed, and then were slightly taken aback as he grabbed our hands and insisted that to pray we must all hold hands. So there we were, sat at a café in the middle of a busy promenade, holding hands and praying with an excitement and passion fuelled by the incredible way God was speaking. I imagine it was quite a sight for bleary-

*eyed revellers on an afternoon-after-the-night-before comedown!
Then without any prompting, Carlos sincerely asked Jesus to come
into his life, to love him, and to help with his problems. It was a very
special moment, which I will never forget.*

*But as amazing as all this was, there was a problem – we still
didn't have long-term structures in place on the island. Carlos had
started a journey with Jesus but, as we were all going home later
that week, we wondered what would happen without us there to
help him along this journey. Would this turn out to be a wasted
moment? Would he get sucked down once again by the troubles of
life?*

*The following summer I returned to Ibiza, and within a couple of
days bumped into Carlos. It turned out that, following a tough
winter, and at the end of himself, Carlos had wandered into a local
church where he met an incredibly generous family who took him
into their home. Carlos was now part of this church, and later that
summer I had the privilege of baptizing him on the beach, with the
rest of the 24-7 community cheering from the water's edge, in front
of countless bemused sun-worshippers. It was another special and
comical Ibiza moment, and God was very present in among the
flaked-out clubbers and topless sunbathers. Carlos is now a legal
migrant, and works as a missionary with surfers.*

The next episode

We left the island that summer asking ourselves what would come
next for 24-7 Prayer in Ibiza. The previous few years had been life-
changing for all of us, but deep down there was a nagging sense we
needed to work out how to sustain a different, yet complementary,
Christian community on the island – one that would be able to love
and to reach out into club culture in the long term. Many of us were
just finishing university or experiencing other life changes that
meant it might not be possible to return for another summer season.

As we wrestled with how to push things to the next level, it
became apparent there really did need to be a shift towards establishing a permanent 24-7 community, to build upon the foundations

laid over the last few years. Meanwhile God was quietly calling several people from within the wider 24-7 Prayer movement to leave behind all that was familiar to them, and to establish this permanent community in Ibiza. So, in the spring of 2005, Brian and Tracy Heasley (with their children, Dan and Ellis) followed God's call and moved to Ibiza. Together with the others who joined them, the Heasleys have firmly established themselves into Ibicenco life, made many friends, and settled into the ebb and flow of the passing seasons – continuing to play, pray and obey within the fast and furious pace of the mad summers, then resting and recuperating in the slower-paced, lazy hazy days of winter.

The permanent 24-7 Ibiza community have earned the respect of the locals, the bar and club owners, the British seasonal-worker community, and just about every other group you could mention. This is down to them living Christ-centred lives, being real, totally committing themselves to serving Ibiza and all who live and travel there, and having a whole lot of fun along the way. They have also established a permanent prayer base in the heart of San Antonio's West End. In their first summer season they received well over 1,000 prayer requests from workers, clubbers and their new-found friends – and have faithfully prayed for each one. Their permanent presence is a constant reminder that Ibiza really is much more than glossy images and hedonistic pursuits; that it is a significant island with a purpose and a destiny; that it is a place and people that God truly loves and is deeply interested in. Their community is a constant reminder that one really can love life, love Jesus, and party with the best of them!

On behalf of everyone who has been part of the 24-7 Prayer team in Ibiza over the years, Vicky would like to dedicate this chapter to Norma, a faithful friend who loved and served the team beyond the call of duty. Norma died in February 2008, after a long battle with cancer.

16
Where do we go from here?

JON OLIVER

I'm going to let you in on a little secret: I'm scared stiff of putting this book together, of setting in stone (or rather, in print) that which should, by its very nature, remain fluid, flexible, free.

I think one of the great dangers we face in developing new strategies for mission is that they can so easily be turned into mere models. The church has a tendency, upon finding a good idea, to turn it into an easily marketable model that can be packaged and promoted, ready to be 'transplanted' into a new setting. This is not to say these models won't work in a different setting but, just as with human transplants, we first need to discern whether the donor material is suitable for the new context. On the whole, I think we would be wise to resist the tendency to make absolutes of that which is inherently transitory – what is appropriate for today might not be tomorrow; what is fitting for one town might not be for another; and what is right for a certain group of people could well be wrong for a whole different group.

There's a bit of me that would love to be able to offer a profound and extensive explanation detailing the way forward for mission in club culture and the nightlife, but I don't think it would actually be helpful. In fact, I don't think it would even be *possible*. This is why

I wanted to gather together so many different stories, so we could catch a glimpse of the enormous diversity out there, and be encouraged and challenged to realize that we can all creatively imagine a new way forward in our own context.

Common themes

As I began to read through these chapters, however, I realized there were several common themes threading their way through the pages, and it occurred to me these could be hinting at the direction we might consider taking. Throughout these stories, I consistently saw a genuine commitment to prayer, accountability, integrity, and relying on God's strength rather than our own. I saw a willingness to try things out, to experiment and creatively explore, and to engage with the mission of God in all sorts of different ways. I saw the importance of caring for people holistically, of genuinely listening to their stories, and of serving and loving people unconditionally. I also saw a real joy in celebrating God's creation, valuing club culture as an expression of our humanity, and enjoying its positive elements to the full – especially the dancing!

In particular, I noticed that almost all the stories were rooted in community – whether this was a group of Christian friends serving together, a team gathered for a specific purpose, a small mission-community, or an established church congregation. Through choice or necessity, some people ended up working by themselves in the nightlife, but they're often the first to acknowledge the importance of being rooted in a meaningful church community. It is here that we find the support and guidance we need to find our way, and the loving encouragement necessary to sustain us on the journey. And it is into this community that we can most effectively welcome those we encounter who are seeking after God. Just as God's mission flows from the heart of the Trinity, so our participation in mission should flow from the heart of the church. As Robert Warren says, 'For too long the church has heard the call of Jesus Christ to become "fishers of men" within the notion of the individualism of rod and line. He addressed that call rather to a group who worked with nets.'[36]

Of course, this isn't the whole story. These are just a few of my reflections, shaped by my own experiences and perspectives. I'm sure you can find various other themes in these chapters that are particularly helpful to you. I hope you do. Let me know. None of us have found *the* way forward; we have each simply found *a* way. My hope is that you will find *your own* way to engage in this great big adventure of mission. Whatever any of us decide to do, it seems clear that we will need to be constantly looking out for the movement of God, remaining flexible and alert for new ways of reaching out to people and impacting the culture around us. I once heard this journey compared to travelling up on a down-escalator – we cannot stay still, but must keep moving to avoid going backwards. I am convinced that our shared story will not be one of conforming to models, but one of continually re-evaluating, reforming and reframing our mission strategy in the light of Jesus' ministry – in the pages of the Bible, in history, and in the world around us.

A five-stage model

On which note, it may be a surprise that I've come up with a little model of my own. I know it sounds as if I don't like models very much, but I do actually think models can be of tremendous value; it's only if we rely on them over and above the prompting of the Spirit that they can become damaging and restrictive. Through reading our stories, my hope is that you might be inspired to join in with this mission too; and, as this may mean developing your own project, I thought it would be helpful to offer you a few tips for getting started. So here I have sketched out a loose framework to help you through the various stages you may need to negotiate in conceiving, growing and developing your own plan for engaging with God's mission in club culture and the nightlife:

Stage 1 CONCEPTION

This is the fun bit, where people come together and something beautiful happens; where new life is breathed into being.

Gathering with others interested in reaching out within club culture, praying together, eating together, sharing together, coming up with ideas, dreams, schemes, visions and possibilities. At this stage, almost no suggestion, however improbable it might seem, should be discounted – in time it may prove to hold the seed of a truly great idea. You'll need to get yourselves out and about in the nightlife, because this is the only way you'll get a feel for what's going on. Here you will begin to get to know yourselves and one another better, and get a glimpse of the adventure ahead. You are limited only by your imagination. But remember this is not just about figuring out what *you* want to do, but about prayerfully discerning what God is doing and how he wants you to partner him in this.

Some questions you might like to ask yourselves:

- Who do we know who might be interested in getting involved?
- What gifts and abilities do we bring as a group?
- What are our hopes and dreams for the project?
- What can we see God doing within the local club scene?
- How can we best serve people, and what needs can we meet?

Stage 2 PREGNANCY

This is when things tend to get a little more complicated, when you've come up with a plan and you're getting ready for action – making preparations, speaking to people who have experience in similar areas, working out how everything will fit together, and through it all continuing to pray and seek God. This will be a time of getting ready for change, and making change. At this stage you might need to nab all sorts of things from other people, groups or congregations – money, ideas, people, premises, resources, whatever. (That's one of the advantages of being part of such a big family, there are always loads of people you can scrounge off!) This is a time of finding balance. Still dreaming big dreams, but also finalizing little details – although if you wait until you've got everything ready, you might never get going. You need to walk the line between maintaining good stewardship and trusting in the Spirit.

Some questions you might like to ask yourselves:

- Are there any other Christians already involved in the local club scene?
- Have we tried to form appropriate links with other church communities?
- Have we liaised with the different agencies already working within the nightlife?
- Will we need any special equipment, and do we need to raise any funding?
- Should we arrange training for people getting involved?
- Do we need specific policies or management and accountability structures in place?
- Do we need to publicize the work?

Stage 3 BIRTH

There will be sweat, there could be tears, there may even be blood, but at the end of the day hopefully something beautiful will be born. This is the stage where all your hard work and preparation pays off. But don't be surprised if it doesn't go as planned. This is mission to a culture that's in transition, and it's likely very little will turn out quite as you might have expected. Whatever it is that you've decided to do, you'll probably want to make sure you're prepared well in advance – not only for those things you've planned, but also ensuring provision for unexpected eventualities. As they say, we need to work as if everything depends on us, and pray as if everything depends on God. Whatever happens, you needn't worry – just remember God's in charge, and that wherever you find yourselves, Jesus has gone before you.

Some questions you might like to ask yourselves:

- Have we got everything prepared as best we can?
- Have we got a contingency plan for when things don't go as expected?
- Are we ready for the long haul?

Stage 4 CHILDHOOD

This is the main event – when you see your 'child', your project, come into its own and develop a wonderful and distinctive character of its very own. What will this look like? I can't tell you that – just as God makes every child unique, so each different project will develop in its own distinctive ways. However, I can tell you that if everything goes well, you'll see the signs of God moving in the world, you'll witness him touching and transforming lives, you'll see people coming to faith, you'll be challenged in ways you never expected, presented with God-given solutions to seemingly impossible situations, and through it all you'll grow ever closer to God. But make sure you're ready for the endless days and sleepless nights! Pray without ceasing, give thanks to God in everything, and remember that once your project gets going it's not a finished product. Just as a child will pick up and discard new hobbies and pastimes, so with your project things will constantly change, people will move on, you'll face new challenges, have new ideas, take the work in new directions.

Some questions you might like to ask yourselves:

- As time goes on, are we still taking care of one another?
- Are we still maintaining accountability?
- Have we kept the local Christian community updated about the work?
- How will we mentor and disciple people as they come to faith?

Stage 5 ADULTHOOD

A good parent knows when it's time to let their child fly the nest. For you, this could mean letting one project wind down in favour of another, or moving on and handing over responsibility to others. You may still be around to offer help and advice, but you have to let people make their own mistakes. You might think you know better, but you need to let people and projects develop in their own ways and in their own time. You have to trust them, and trust the Holy Spirit to guide them. When God says it's time to let go, you really do need to. This could even mean letting the project come to an end. That's OK! Sometimes we can become so focused on growth and stability that we feel we've failed if things come to an end – but sometimes this is precisely what needs to happen. It may be difficult, but when it's time to move on, you really do need to move on.

Some questions you might like to ask yourselves:

- Are we still seeking God, or just going through the motions?
- Does God want to take us in new directions?
- Are people being suitably trained and discipled to take over the work?
- Am I ready to hand over the reins, or to have the reins handed over to me?
- Am I prepared to let the whole thing come to an end?

Remember, though, that this model is only an illustration, a rough sketch, a few suggestions. It hasn't even always worked out this way for me – so take from it what you will. If it fits, put it on. If it doesn't, put it back down again.

Plan B

On the other hand, you could just go clubbing!

You see, despite all the different schemes and stories, ideas and inspirations, projects and plans we can find in this book, sometimes I still think the best thing is simply to get in there and see what happens. See where God is moving. See where he takes you in this great big adventure of his. No great mission strategy can replace the incredible impact of simply being on hand when God is at work.

When I first started out as a nightclub chaplain, I got to know several other Christians already involved in the club scene – DJs, clubbers, bar-staff, bouncers, all sorts. Although some of these people got involved with the chaplaincy, I was keen not to undermine the importance of their existing witness within the nightlife, nor to draw them away from their current contexts, where they had already developed countless friendships and seen many opportunities in which they could witness to the good news. After all, it seemed foolish to draw them away from their present environment, only to have them work with us to try and do the same thing from scratch. Instead our hope was to encourage and support them where they already were. I still think this was the right move, because at the heart of mission is the simple call for Christians to engage in all levels and every aspect of our culture. God is at work in the world, and he wants us to be right in there with him.

If you feel called to something more structured, though, to develop a more formal project or a more focused approach, my model may offer you some pointers. But if you simply enjoy clubbing, or if you're involved in club culture in any other way, you shouldn't feel you have to get involved with some sort of grand scheme or new project. You might still want to ask yourself some of the questions above, as you prayerfully discern where God is moving and taking you, but it may well be you're already in the place where God wants you. Similarly, if you've got friends who go clubbing, but you've shied away from joining them in the past, then perhaps getting in alongside them is precisely what God wants you to do. The strategy is simple: to demonstrate the good news as best you can with your words, your actions, your attitudes, your compassion and your generosity of spirit; to love, serve and meet the needs of the people you come across; to strive to bring out the God-flavours and God-colours in the world; and to be ready at all times to offer an explanation for the hope you have in Jesus.

'Don't begin by travelling to some far-off place to convert un-believers. And don't try to be dramatic by tackling some public enemy. Go to the lost, confused people right here in the neighbour-hood. Tell them that the kingdom is here. Bring health to the sick. Raise the dead. Touch the untouchables. Kick out the demons. You have been treated generously, so live generously. Don't think you have to put on a fund-raising campaign before you start. You don't need a lot of equipment. You are the equipment, and all you need to keep that going is three meals a day. Travel light' (Matthew 10.5–10, MSG).

On second thoughts, maybe I should have called this section 'Plan A', because it seems to me that this is just as important, if not more so, than the most ingenious strategies for mission. Clubbers simply clubbing. Being Christians in the world. And this doesn't just apply to club culture – whatever it is that you're into (skateboarding, snowboarding, surfing, stamp-collecting, bird-watching, caravanning, football, cycling, cinema), whatever it is you're passionate about, whatever it is that flows out from within, it may be that this is part of who God has made you to be, that this is where God has called you to be, and that this is how God is beckoning you to join in with his great flowing mission in and towards the world.

Where do we go from here?

So where do we go from here? To be honest, I'm not sure. I haven't worked it all out. I haven't got a foolproof blueprint for success. This isn't the 'teacher's edition' with the answers hidden away at the back! This is simply part of our journey of discovery, part of our ongoing attempt to discern what God is doing in the world, and how he might be calling us to partner him in his mission.

One thing that has become increasingly clear to me is that as we continue on this journey we will most likely need to see new forms of church developing within club culture. As we continue to see faith blossom and God touching people's lives, we will need to explore new ways of discipling people, of partnering God to see people grow in their journey of faith – because some people simply won't fit into the church as it currently stands . . . Wait! That makes it sound as if the blame lies squarely with the newcomers. Perhaps I should have said that the existing forms of church won't fit some people who may otherwise be interested in forming a relationship with Jesus.

Over the years we have developed our own culture in the church; our own ways of doing things, certain expectations of behaviour, particular manners of dress and speech, unspoken rules, formulaic rituals – and in doing so we have dressed up the gospel in these cultural trappings. To a certain extent this is healthy, because by giving it our own slant, our own edge, this is how we come to understand the gospel for ourselves – but in doing so we must be careful not to confuse our own church culture with the gospel.

We cannot assume that our way of doing things is the only way.

We can't take it for granted that we've somehow got everything right and club culture (or any other culture) has got it all wrong. We must not try to sell our way of doing things, disguised as the good news. This is what the first-century Christians tried to do when they insisted that converts had to undergo circumcision in order to be accepted into the community of believers (Galatians 6.12–16; 1 Corinthians 7.17–20), and we need to avoid making the same type of mistake today. Although the church no longer insists on circumcision, sadly we sometimes still insist that if people are interested in faith, they need to have two conversions – one into Christianity and one into our culture. The danger here is that if these people reject our culture, our way of doing things, they may also reject the gospel – they may inadvertently reject Christ.

If we hope to see people coming to faith from within club culture, we cannot assume they will fit comfortably into our existing church structures. Some people will, some people won't. This is not to say there is necessarily anything wrong with our current forms of church, but simply that we may be called to explore the possibilities of alternative ways of being and doing church that are more accessible to people from outside our traditions. Not to replace the existing church, but to complement it. As Jesus said, 'No one sews a patch of unshrunk cloth on an old garment, for the patch will pull away from the garment, making the tear worse. Neither do people pour new wine into old wineskins. If they do, the skins will burst; the wine will run out, and the wineskins will be ruined. No, they pour new wine into new wineskins, and both are preserved' (Matthew 9.16–17). I can't say what these new wineskins, these new forms and fresh expressions of church, will look like – because we're unlikely to be able to discern their form until they come into being. This subject deserves another whole book of its own (in fact, this already is the subject of countless other books*), but for now the question we need to ask ourselves is: 'Are we going to be prepared to encourage and enable these new wineskins as they emerge within club culture?'

This may not be something that we are all entirely comfortable with, it may make us feel uneasy or unsettled – but Jesus never said

---

* Check out the Recommended Reading section at the end of the book for a selection of my own favourites.

anything about being comfortable or getting settled. If anything, he said the reverse. Jesus consistently unsettled people when he walked the earth, has continued to do so throughout history, and still has the power to shake us up today as he calls us into new and uncertain places. One thing that does seem certain is that if we want new wine, we'll probably need new wineskins. As Leonard Sweet suggests, 'Every generation needs a shape that fits its own hands, its own soul. Each generation, every person, needs a different handle from which to receive the living waters of Jesus. Our task is to pour the living water into anything anyone will pick up . . . I must be prepared to pour the living water into containers out of which I myself would never be caught dead drinking.'[37]

17

Are we nearly there yet?

JON OLIVER

The other day a friend of mine told me how much he hates the 'mission board' on the wall at his local church – you know the sort, a big map of the world radiating multicoloured bits of wool from various foreign countries out to all the smiley photos of people scattered around it. He says that somehow we've got the idea into our heads that mission is something that happens elsewhere, overseas, or at least in some distant part of our own country. And is it any wonder this false impression has seeped into our consciousness when we have these 'mission boards' reinforcing the misconception, when we have 'mission reports' about the people 'out there' who we're supporting, and when we only ever really call people 'missionaries' if they're overseas?

So my friend reckons they should either get rid of the map, or invest in a new camera and a huge bag of wool – then smother the whole place with photos of absolutely everyone, with countless little threads of wool trailing their way around the building and back to the map. Leading to every single place where every single member of the congregation lives/works/socializes; every single place in which they are called to be; to the very places where each and every one of them is called to be a missionary.

The missionary journey

A missionary is simply someone who is engaging with the mission of God in a particular context. This could be anywhere. This should be everywhere. This journey has taken some of us into club culture and the nightlife. I don't know where this journey might take you. Maybe you know, maybe you don't; maybe you're already there. You probably are. It could be club culture, or it could be somewhere else entirely. It could be where you live, where you work, or where you play. It could be where you find yourself naturally, or where you put yourself deliberately for the sake of mission. It could be all of the above. The simple fact is that, as Christians, every single one of us is called to be a missionary, to engage in mission wherever we find ourselves.

So what is mission? First and foremost, mission is God's movement in and towards the world. Beyond this, I am wary of trying to define mission too rigidly because, as our stories have shown, the missionary call is so wide-reaching and multi-faceted that it cannot easily be defined. But I'll give it a go: mission is the ongoing work of Jesus among his people, empowered by the Spirit, and directed towards the whole world. Mission lives in the spaces between the past and the future of God's people, and between the existing communities of faith and those outside them. Mission includes, but is not limited to, evangelism. Mission seeks wholeness of being, concerning both physical and spiritual salvation. Mission transcends our individual cultural concerns, and shapes itself in relation to the culture in which it finds itself. Mission involves proclaiming the good news and redressing injustice, nurturing new believers and caring for creation, participating in evangelism and responding to human need through loving service.[38] Mission encompasses and interacts with almost every other aspect of faith – our understanding of God, worship, prayer, justice, love, relationships, social action, and the very nature of the church itself. As Vincent Donovan says, 'Mission is the meaning of the church. The church can only exist insofar as it is in mission, insofar as it participates in the act of Christ, which is mission . . . Without this mission, there would be no church.'[39]

Through all this, I am consistently reminded that mission is about so much more than simply seeking converts. I remain convinced this is a key element of mission, but nonetheless I have deliberately decided not to mention how many people I've seen become Christians, because in some ways that's not the point. The walk of faith is a journey, a gradual process, which often begins a long time before a commitment of faith is made, and which hopefully continues long afterwards. So surely our focus needs to be on the long term, on the direction we're travelling rather than the place where we currently stand. All too often we concentrate almost exclusively on whether people are 'inside' or 'outside' the church – and I sometimes wonder if it would be better if we focused instead on whether people are moving 'towards' or 'away from' God. It is entirely possible that some people inside the church are actually moving away from God, while some people outside the church are steadily moving towards him.[40] The moment when a twenty-something clubber, who had seemingly never given a single thought to the existence of God, stopped to consider the possibility that there might be something more than the material world; the moment when a lad who believed in God, but didn't know Christ, asked me to pray with him and asked Jesus to make himself known; the moment when someone I'd met just a few weeks before decided to follow Jesus; the moment when one of my Christian volunteers experienced God afresh and took a step closer – all of these moments are part of this same wonderful movement towards God.

Stumbling towards the future

Sometimes when I tell people about my work, it's all too easy to focus entirely on these kinds of stories, on these wonderful signs of God at work within club culture, and to overlook the long days and endless nights when we face setbacks, make mistakes, and seem to get nowhere. It's also easy to focus entirely on my hopes and dreams, and to inadvertently share my vision for the future as if it were our present reality. This is why we have tried to offer our experiences warts and all, rather than presenting some projected or idealized version of events. These are simply our stories, a few things that a handful of people have seen and done – and, as these pages show, we have all faced our fair share of success and failure. In fact, I specifically asked the others not to cover over their mistakes, as I feel these are a vital part of our stories – because it won't always be easy and we won't always get things right. Our hope and prayer is that these explorations and experiments will work out for the best in the long term, but we have to face the fact that we'll inevitably make mistakes along the way, and mustn't let fear prevent us from ever taking a risk.

We've all made mistakes – whether it's making misguided decisions, trying to push the work in wrong directions, developing projects way off the mark, relying on our own strength rather than God's (or the support of the community around us), failing to provide adequate signposts, or even temporarily forgetting why we set out on this adventure in the first place. I for one have made more than my fair share of mistakes, not least in starting up a number of projects that have fallen flat on their faces – the club night we ran for a while was a financial disaster, the team we tried to take into one of the clubs just didn't come together properly, and although we have a great website, my attempts at starting up a community web-forum failed dismally.

Even with the projects that *have* worked out, I've still sometimes made mistakes. There have been occasions when I've said things I shouldn't have, and others when I've said nothing when I should have said something. At times I've walked on by when maybe I should have intervened, and sometimes I've stuck my nose in where it simply wasn't wanted. Just a few weeks before I finished writing this book, I foolishly walked into a very nasty situation that had just spilled out of a particularly notorious nightclub – and ended up with a broken nose, a faceful of cuts and bruises, and a week-long concussion. As I sat there on the street corner, bleeding profusely and utterly shaken, I had to ask myself, 'Did I do wrong? Could I have taken more care, shown more caution? Should I have walked by on the other side?' I still don't know.

Sometimes it's obvious right away when I've made a mistake; sometimes I don't realize until a long time afterwards; and sometimes I'm just not sure. There's one situation in particular that still bothers me from time to time. Over the last few years I've got to know some of the staff at one of the local strip clubs, and they've often invited me in to have a drink and a chat on their turf. I have always refused. This is one of my boundaries. It is a boundary that I'm comfortable with, and on the whole I feel I've made the right decision. But every now and then I wonder, 'What would have happened if I'd gone in, if I'd accepted this invitation into their world?' After all, did I not trust that God would have gone before me, that Jesus could have worked through me? I've been thinking about this a lot recently, especially since I heard the incredible and unlikely story of an Australian evangelist who accidentally accepted a desperate invitation from an exotic dancer to meet in the strip club where she worked. Realizing all too late where they had arranged to meet, and with no other way of contacting her, he eventually resolved to go along to the strip club – where they chatted for a long time, before he ended up leading her to Christ right there in the middle of the club.[41] I still don't think I'll be accepting any invitations to a strip club any time soon – but this story has certainly challenged me to remember that God will never be confined by my boundaries, and that I must always rely on his guiding hand rather than my own assumptions in where he is at work.

This means the journey won't always be comfortable, and that there will be all sorts of dangers along the way – but, as far as I'm concerned, it's worth the risk. This is life in all its fullness; its ups and downs, its successes and failures, its breathtaking highs and inevitable lows. Making mistakes is not the problem; the real problem is letting those mistakes trick us into giving up. We all make mistakes. I certainly have. I've made some absolute blunders. But when I get things wrong, I pick myself up, brush myself down, and try again. There's always hope. I think that we only ever really fail if we give up trying.

Are we nearly there yet?

I often find myself asking what the next step will be, where we'll go from here, where we'll find ourselves this time next year – but, as

183

I've already said, I just don't know. I *do* know that it won't always be easy – that there will be risks and temptations, failures and disappointments – but I also know that if God is for us, nothing can stand against us. As Graham Cray says, 'Some cultures may prove harder for the church to connect with than others, but none are harder for the Holy Spirit.'[42]

Are we there yet? No, of course not. As you've seen, some people have been involved in this sort of work for ages and have barely begun to see any fruit. But this isn't a hit-and-run mission strategy, and we need to be prepared to be in it for the long haul if we hope to see any lasting transformation. On the one hand, mission in club culture and the nightlife is largely uncharted territory for the church, but on the other, this process of engaging in the unpredictable mission of God is the very same thing the church has been doing throughout its entire history – creatively re-imagining how we can effectively communicate the gospel to people from every nation, tribe and tongue. If God's mission is like an open river, flowing this way and that, breaking its banks and overflowing in unexpected places, the question we have to ask ourselves is: 'Have we got enough courage to face our fears, throw caution to the wind, and dive in headlong?'[43]

As we reach the end of the book I'd like to consider the story of Moses sending the spies into the Promised Land (Numbers 13–14). In this story we find that the majority of the spies returned fearful, claiming that the land was populated by giants and impossible to conquer. Joshua and Caleb, however, returned confident that the rich and fertile land could be taken with a little ingenuity and a lot of help from God. Presented with this choice, and concerned for their own safety, the Israelites chose trepidation and were relegated to wandering the barren desert for 40 years.[44]

Poised on the edge of a new and equally frightening frontier, we are faced with a similar choice in our own time – to shy away in fear from the challenge set before us, or to confront it head-on with

Caleb's confidence. I firmly believe that God is beckoning his people to join him now in this great big adventure of mission within the rich and fertile landscape of club culture and the nightlife – and I for one am not going to spend the next 40 years wandering aimlessly in the desert. I'd rather be killed by giants.

Epilogue

Of course, the story doesn't end here – if you want to find out more, if you want to connect with people involved in this adventure of mission in your own area, if you want to contact those who have contributed their stories to this book, or if you've got your own stories of mission in club culture and the nightlife to share – log on at

www.night-vision.org

Notes

1 The Mission of God

1 David Bosch, *Transforming Mission*, p. 228.
2 Jürgen Moltmann, *The Church in the Power of the Spirit*, p. 64.
3 David Bosch, *Transforming Mission*, p. 390.
4 Emil Brunner, *The Word and the World*, p. 108.
5 Michael Riddell, *Threshold of the Future*, p. 18.
6 Dave Tomlinson, *The Post-Evangelical*, p. 143.
7 Cathy Kirkpatrick *et al.*, *The Prodigal Project*, p. 126.

2 Salt and Light

8 Ray Oldenburg, *The Great Good Place*.
9 Michael Frost, *Exiles: Living Missionally in a Post-Christian Culture*, p. 57.
10 Michael Frost, *Exiles: Living Missionally in a Post-Christian Culture*, p. 58.
11 Michael Frost, *Exiles: Living Missionally in a Post-Christian Culture*, p. 59.
12 Mintel Reports, *Late Licensing – UK*.
13 Home Office, *Calculating the Risk*.
14 Peter Brierley, *The Tide is Running Out*, p. 99.
15 Quoted in Jonathan Petre, 'Nightclub Chaplain Spreads Gospel of Lord of the Dance', in *The Daily Telegraph* (19 June 2001).
16 John Stott, *The Message of the Sermon on the Mount*.
17 Tony Campolo, quoted in Dave Tomlinson, *The Post-Evangelical*, p. 43.
18 Michael Riddell, *Threshold of the Future*, p. 18.

3 Spirituality of the Age

19 Pete Greig and Dave Roberts, *Red Moon Rising*, p. 250.

20 John Mbiti, in Tony Lane, *The Lion Book of Christian Thought*, p. 249.

21 Ben Malbon, *Clubbing: Dancing, Ecstasy and Vitality*, pp. 106–9.

22 Gordon Lynch and Emily Badger, 'The Mainstream Post-Rave Club Scene as a Secondary Institution', in *Culture and Religion*, vol. 7, no. 1, p. 27.

23 John Drane, *What is the New Age Saying to the Church?*, p. 239.

24 Phil Rankin, *Buried Spirituality*, p. 80.

25 Phil Rankin, *Buried Spirituality*, pp. 80–1.

26 Sara Savage *et al.*, *Making Sense of Generation Y*, p. 37.

27 Ann Morisy, quoted in Graham Cray, 'Reconnecting with Generation Y – and all those like them', in Sara Savage *et al.*, *Making Sense of Generation Y*, p. 162.

28 Graham Cray, 'Reconnecting with Generation Y – and all those like them', in Sara Savage *et al.*, *Making Sense of Generation Y*, pp. 162–9.

29 Graham Cray, 'Reconnecting with Generation Y – and all those like them', in Sara Savage *et al.*, *Making Sense of Generation Y*, p. 162.

30 See Luke 10.25–37; Matthew 25.31–46; Luke 4.16–21.

7 The Malt Cross

31 Vincent Donovan, *Christianity Rediscovered*, p. xix.

12 Talking Space

32 Vincent Donovan, *Christianity Rediscovered*, p. 14.

33 Vincent Donovan, *Christianity Rediscovered*, p. 75.

13 Church for the Night

34 dfg, 'The King's Arms', from the album *you are the problem, dfg is the solution*. (Reproduced with permission. All rights reserved.)

35 Cathy Kirkpatrick *et al.*, *The Prodigal Project*, p. 63.

16 Where Do We Go from Here?

36 Robert Warren, *Being Human, Being Church*, p. 156.

37 Leonard Sweet, *Aqua Church*, p. 29.

17 Are We Nearly There Yet?

38 These last few are adapted from the 'Five Marks of Mission', in The Archbishops' Council, *Mission-Shaped Church*, pp. 81–156.

39 Vincent Donovan, *Christianity Rediscovered*, p. 82.

40 Michael Riddell, *Threshold of the Future*, p. 152.

41 This full story can be found in Michael Frost and Alan Hirsch, *The Shaping of Things to Come*, pp. 159–61.

42 Graham Cray, 'Reconnecting with Generation Y – and all those like them', in Sara Savage *et al.*, *Making Sense of Generation Y*, p. 157.

43 Michael Riddell, *Threshold of the Future*, p. 18.

44 Michael Riddell, *Threshold of the Future*, p. 15.

Recommended Reading and Bibliography

Recommended reading

There are so many great books I couldn't possibly list them all, but if you're interested in exploring the possibilities of church and mission within contemporary society, here's a small selection of my favourites to help get you started:

Mission-Shaped Church, by The Archbishops' Council
This book goes some way to proving Gavin Tyte's suggestion that the Church of England is an incredibly innovative and creative force (see Chapter 14), as it explores a whole variety of fresh new ways in which church is being expressed all across the UK. However, this is not just about the Church of England, but instead offers a profound challenge to all of us to creatively consider how we can develop mission-shaped communities that will effectively connect with people currently outside the church.

Transforming Mission, by David Bosch
This book is frighteningly long, and sits bigger than some of the Bibles on my bookshelf – but, after the Bible, it's probably the most interesting and comprehensive book about mission that you could

ever get your hands on. So why not get your hands on a copy? Seriously, do it. It's absolutely amazing.

Christianity Rediscovered, by Vincent Donovan

This is the truly inspiring story of a Catholic priest who travelled to Tanzania to be a missionary among the Masai, and ended up having everything he thought he knew about mission and evangelism questioned in the process. Published over 30 years ago, this book still has the power to challenge anyone involved in mission today – especially those interested in the relationship between the gospel and culture.

Exiles: Living Missionally in a Post-Christian Culture, by Michael Frost

This book contains a good deal of pointed critique about the church as we know it, which could well offend some people, but it's also jam-packed with real-life stories of people creatively engaged in God's mission within contemporary society – offering signs of hope and inspiration for anyone who longs to live an authentic life of mission as a follower of Christ in the ever-changing world around us. (If you like this one, you might also want to look out for *The Shaping of Things to Come*, by Michael Frost and Alan Hirsch.)

Red Moon Rising, by Pete Greig and Dave Roberts

This is the story of the beginning of an adventure – of the accidental founding of 24-7 Prayer in a small room in Chichester, its growth into a worldwide prayer movement, and its continued development as a prayerful mission community. I loved it! (And it comes highly recommended by many of the people who contributed their stories to this book.)

Clubbing: Dancing, Ecstasy and Vitality, by Ben Malbon

This book is about clubbing. Plain and simple. It is largely based on the author's own PhD research and is very much an academic work, but it's actually a lot more accessible than I first assumed – particularly as it's peppered throughout with real-life stories from clubbers he interviewed and little snippets from his own nights out. Although it's deeply rooted in a review of club culture from the late 90s, it still provides a compelling insight into the world of clubbers and clubbing.

Threshold of the Future, by Mike Riddell

Mike Riddell has written some of the most interesting, profound, challenging and, at times, uncomfortable books that I've read about church and mission. There are loads to choose from, including *The Prodigal Project* (which he co-authored with Cathy Kirkpatrick *et al.*) and the bizarrely-titled *alt.spirit@metro.m3*, but this one is definitely my favourite – not least because I am continually inspired by the illustration of God's mission being like an open river. Well worth a look.

Being Human, Being Church, by Robert Warren

This book looks at how we engage in community, worship and mission, and suggests that the heartbeat of the church exists where these three areas overlap. I had to keep stopping while I was reading so I could underline countless different passages – and in the end I think there might have been more text underlined than not!

And finally, if you're really keen, you might want to track down a copy of *Culture and Religion* from March 2006 (your best bet is probably to have a look in the nearest university library). This is a special issue of the journal edited by Graham St John, who gathered together six articles focused on 'Electronic Dance Music Culture and Religion'. To be honest, reading some of these articles made my head hurt, but don't let that put you off – as it provides an incredibly interesting and in-depth analysis of the 'spiritual' and 'religious' aspects of club culture, stretching back as far as the rave scene of the late 80s and the free festivals of the 70s.

Bibliography

Archbishops' Council, *Mission-Shaped Church*, Church House Publishing, London, 2004.

Bosch, David, *Transforming Mission*, Orbis Books, New York, 1991.

Brierley, Peter, *The Tide is Running Out*, Christian Research, Swindon, 2000.

Brunner, Emil, *The Word and the World*, Charles Scribner's Sons, New York, 1931.

Cray, Graham, 'Reconnecting with Generation Y – and all those like them', in Savage, Sara *et al.*, *Making Sense of Generation Y*, Church House Publishing, London, 2006.

dfg, 'The King's Arms', from the album *you are the problem, dfg is the solution*, Sticky Music, Glasgow, 2003.

Donovan, Vincent, *Christianity Rediscovered – Third Edition*, SCM Press, London, 2001.

Drane, John, *What is the New Age Saying to the Church?*, Marshall Pickering, London, 1991.

Frost, Michael, *Exiles: Living Missionally in a Post-Christian Culture*, Hendrickson Publishers, Massachusetts, 2006.

Frost, Michael, and Hirsch, Alan, *The Shaping of Things to Come*, Hendrickson Publishers, Massachusetts, 2003.

Greig, Pete, and Roberts, Dave, *Red Moon Rising*, Kingsway Publications, Eastbourne, 2004.

Home Office, *Calculating the Risk*, Crown Copyright, London, 2003.

Kirkpatrick, Cathy *et al.*, The Prodigal Project, SPCK, London, 2000.

Lane, Tony, *The Lion Book of Christian Thought*, Lion Publishing, Oxford, 1992.

Lynch, Gordon, and Badger, Emily, 'The Mainstream Post-Rave Club Scene as a Secondary Institution', in *Culture and Religion*, vol. 7, no. 1 (March 2006), pp. 27–40.

Malbon, Ben, *Clubbing: Dancing, Ecstasy and Vitality*, Routledge, Abingdon, 1999.

Mintel Reports, *Late Licensing – UK*, Mintel International Group, London, 2005.

Moltmann, Jürgen, *The Church in the Power of the Spirit*, SCM Press, London, 1977.

Oldenburg, Ray, *The Great Good Place*, Paragon House, New York, 1989.

Petre, Jonathan, 'Nightclub Chaplain Spreads Gospel of Lord of the Dance', in *The Daily Telegraph* (19 June 2001), Telegraph Media Group, London, 2001.

Rankin, Phil, *Buried Spirituality*, Sarum College Press, Salisbury, 2005.

Riddell, Michael, *Threshold of the Future*, SPCK, London, 1998.

Savage, Sara *et al.*, *Making Sense of Generation Y*, Church House Publishing, London, 2006.

Stott, John, *The Message of the Sermon on the Mount*, Intervarsity Press, Illinois, 1978.

Sweet, Leonard, *Aqua Church*, Group Publishing, Colorado, 1999.

Tomlinson, Dave, *The Post-Evangelical*, Triangle, London, 1995.

Ward, Pete, *Liquid Church*, Paternoster Press, Carlisle, 2002.

Warren, Robert, *Being Human, Being Church*, Marshall Pickering, London, 1995